The Shoe-Leather Globe

(Continued from front flap)

vivid details of these give glimpses into life in eighteenth-century England and India. Also portrayed are some of the problems and hardships experienced by early missionaries to India.

To the young reader, it will give joy that the "Father of Modern Protestant Missions" was once a boy who played kickball and kept tadpoles on a window shelf.

About the Author

For several years Saxon Rowe Carver served with her husband as a missionary to China. She taught for 11 years in the University of Shanghai.

Returning to this country she worked as a school and church librarian. A recent trip back to the Orient included teaching for a year in Hong Kong Baptist College.

This is Mrs. Carver's third contribution to Broadman's Junior Biography Series. Earlier volumes are *William Colgate, Yeoman of Kent;* and *Ropes to Burma, the Story of Luther Rice.*

THE SHOE-LEATHER
GLOBE
A Life of
WILLIAM CAREY

Saxon Rowe Carver

ILLUSTRATED BY PAUL GRANGER

2740

BROADMAN PRESS
Nashville, Tennessee

424–087

Dewey Decimal Classification: J266.092
Library of Congress Catalog Card Number: 65–19545
Printed in the United States of America
7.5MH65KSP

Contents

To Three Little Boys

1
Up the Tree Again

"You dassn't go up that tree, Will Carey. You'll fall and break your arm again!"

"I dare! 'Twas my own arm, and it's well enough for climbing. See, Willie? See?"

While he argued, Will Carey pulled himself higher into the tree, bare toes curling around the bark. From the ground where Willie Hinde stood fretting, Will's bright yellow smock looked like a rising moon.

"Come down, I say. You mind me. I'm older'n you."

"No, I've got to see if there are baby robins. Stop shouting now, Willie Hinde. I hear cheeps."

Balancing his body carefully, Will inched his way toward the thinner limbs of the old beech tree. Up high, they shook. He paused to steady himself, and as he waited for a moment, he looked across the churchyard toward his own cottage.

From Will's tree perch, his own house looked tiny, sitting on its little grassy knoll a bit away from the other houses of the village. In fact, all of Paulerspury looked ever so small, with the gray stone church the biggest thing around. Watling Street, which ran behind the village on its way across all England, was a narrow streak of brown mud.

Now the limbs had stopped swaying, and Will was high enough to look down into the nest. Inside, four baby birds were shoving one another around. Will froze still, for the father robin was diving home with an angleworm in his mouth. Four baby mouths opened incredibly wide. One was quicker, luckier. The other three cried in disappointment. The male bird flew away.

The last time Will had climbed this tree—the day when the limbs were so slippery and he had lost his hold and fallen—he had seen five green-blue eggs. One must have broken in the spring storms. Now Will looked at the four ugly little creatures. He looked and wondered . . .

When will their feathers change to red and brown? How long will it be before they can fly? How much can a baby bird eat in a day?

"Will Carey, I'm tired of telling you." Willie Hinde's high whine from the ground started the mother bird to fussing and beating her wings. "If you don't come down right now I'm going to tell yer mum. She told you to be careful this first day."

"Tell her."

Willie trotted off. Will heard him jump from the stone

wall which enclosed the parish graveyard where the boys were playing, and figured it would take him about three minutes to reach the Carey home. This gave him longer for bird-watching, even if his mother came to fetch him.

Suddenly the big bell in the church tower tolled for noon, and there was commotion in the beech tree. Will jumped, almost falling. The parent robins decided that the boy was the enemy who had made the noise. The visit was over.

Thankful not to be pecked, Will slithered to the ground where his stockings and jackboots lay. He hadn't thought about cold feet, but he had them, and he pulled on his long knitted stockings in a hurry.

While he tugged at his boots, Will wished he had thought to watch the clapper swing when the bell rang. Once he had climbed into the tower, but not at a striking time. Oh, well, another day he would.

A pony cart creaked into the close and stopped at the church door. Old Dick, the squire's gardener, hailed Will from the driver's bench. "Good day t'ye, laddie."

Will rushed to the cart which was ablaze with bloom. He gazed openmouthed at pansies and daffodils, tulips and tall white lilies, even fragrant purple hyacinths, all in pots.

"Whatever are you doing with all those flowers, Old Dick?"

"Tomorrow's Easter Sunday, laddie. The squire sent them to prettify the church."

"But all at once they've blossoms. I've seen not one daf-fodil on the hillside—and I've looked."

"In a few weeks, come May, ye'll see thousands." Old Dick climbed creakily down from the seat of the cart. "It takes skill, me boy, to have them all ready together for the big day—and a fine greenhouse, such as the squire owns."

"Could I ever learn? Will you teach me? Is it hard? How do you know when they are going to bloom?" Will's questions tumbled one upon the other.

"You could learn. You've a liking for growing things, be they creatures or plants. That's a first step. Now, how's to helping me unload? Is the arm up to it?"

Will grinned. "For certain. I've just been up the beech tree. Didn't feel a pull."

Willie Hinde's threat to tell on him was forgotten while Will worked with Old Dick to place the flowers near the altar, lilies at the back, the plants with shorter stems in front. Above the flowers, the pulpit rose high to one side, and beyond it a stained glass window gave soft colored light on to the old pews and bare gray walls.

When the flowers were all in place, Old Dick and Will stood back, caps in hand, to admire the effect.

Old Dick broke the silence with a deep sigh and a shake of his freckled bald head. "She looks fine, she does," he declared. "Tomorrow when folkses walk in and nod to one another with pleasure, we'll feel proud as proud, won't we?"

Will was proud already.

Old Dick went on, as if to himself. "Easter Sunday, year of Our Lord, 1767, seventh year of the reign of His Majesty King George III, God bless him. Can't believe it. Seems yesterday he took the throne. But I'm getting old. The years run together. I get mixed up about time."

"How old are you, Old Dick?"

"Seventy-six, laddie. And still able to do my work, thank God. Think ye could spare me an hour this afternoon, now, to clean around the headstones? After Easter services, our families wander about the graveyard, and there's a sight of bracken and brambles collected since last fall."

"I'd like to help you. And I'll get Willie Hinde, too. I think I know just where he is. You wait, I'll fetch him fast."

"Do that. And after we work a spell, I'll have a treat for us. When I drove off, Cook handed me a fine fat sausage and a chunk of ripe cheese. Think ye could use some?"

Will's round little face lit up when his friend mentioned a treat. His wide smile showed that two front teeth were missing, and the dimple in his chin seemed to be in a straight line from the center gap.

"I'll bring my own rake," he called over his shoulder.

He meant to run all the way home, but when he reached the brook which bubbled its merry way past the close,

Will saw violets on the mossy bank. Quickly he gathered a handful for his mother, then picked up speed again.

Will was not as tall as the thornbush hedge around the Carey's yard. As he neared it, he heard his mother's voice. Sure that Willie had told on him for climbing the tree again, he waited behind the hedge to listen.

"No, Willie, I don't propose to send Mr. Carey to the churchyard. He could never climb that tree, and I'm sure Will is safely down by now. But, tell me, did he take off his boots? They slip."

"Yes, ma'am, he was barefoot. But he still coulda hurt himself, the first day out, and all. I told him and told him to come down . . ."

"Now Willie, let's understand something, between us. You are kind to Will, and being older, you feel that you must look after him. But you don't need to worry so. I want Will to feel free to go about, much as he likes. If he hankers to climb, I choose for him to do so. The day will come, soon enough, when he'll be a weaver, like his father, and have to stay indoors from dawn to dark."

"He did break his arm."

"True. And suffered for it. But no doubt he had to go back up that tree, to prove to himself that he was not afraid. He's a determined lad. Don't you remember how, last summer you and he decided to follow the sheep down Watling Street to the shearing place, and how far it was, and how tired you both were that night?"

"Yes, ma'am. 'Tweren't my fault. I kept telling Will to turn around but he would see that shearing. It was a sight, it was."

Satisfied, Will stood on tiptoe and peeped over the hedge. His mother was forking dirt around a rosebush, and Willie sat on the stone bench beside the door, perspiring. With his brown jerkin pulled loose from his breeches-top and his reddish hair all a-tangle, he presented a comical picture. Will wished that his friend knew how to have fun, and wasn't always fretting about what would happen next.

For a few moments nobody spoke. The thrum, thrum thrum of the loom from an upstairs room where Mr. Carey was weaving was the only sound in the yard. Then Will's five-year-old sister Ann came outside, with a bowl of porridge in her hand. Catching sight of Will's head above the hedge, she shouted "There he is now, Mummy, not hurt at all!"

Will came through the hedge and held out the violets to his mother. She smelled them with delight. For a second, he was afraid she was going to kiss him. Instead, she gave him a smile of thanks and asked whether he was hungry.

"No, ma'am. I've just come for my rake, and to hunt up Willie Hinde. Old Dick wants we should clear bits and bracken from the churchyard. He has sausage and cheese for us when we're done."

Ann began to fidget. She put her porridge bowl down on the bench beside Willie Hinde and begged, "Me, too! Me, too! May I go with Will, Mummy?"

"If he says so."

"Ye-es. She can pick up sticks."

"Well, Ann, if you are going, I want to braid your hair." She drew the little girl to her and plaited her fly-away fair hair into two firm pigtails. Will was glad he didn't have to put up with such nonsense. He went around the cottage to the toolshed for his rake.

Finished with Ann's hair, Mrs. Carey asked Will again whether he didn't want a bite to eat, but he was too eager to get going to stop longer.

"We could take a pasty in our hands," suggested Willie Hinde, and it was settled that way.

"You've already had two, Willie Hinde," declared Ann. "I gave them to you while you waited for Mummy. You eat too much. That's why you're so fat and puffy."

"Be off, all of you," cried Mrs. Carey. "I've got to wind some yarn for Mr. Carey. I promised I'd have it done by night, and there's a great basket of it."

The fat boy, the short one, and the stringy little girl started out the gate, purpose in every step. Then Mrs. Carey called, "Oh, Ann and Will, don't stay too long. I'm going to heat the copper this afternoon. It's all-over baths for everybody before dark. Tomorrow's Easter, don't forget."

2
"I'll Learn to Read!"

On the next morning Will Carey was awakened by the joyous peal of church bells, calling all members of Paulerspury parish to come and worship a risen Lord. He thought of words his mother had used after baths last night: "fresh in body and soul"; and he decided that was the way he felt this Easter morning.

As he lay in bed, Will pictured the ringers at the bell ropes. He knew they were making long pulls, for the bells gave forth such beautiful sounds.

Oatmeal was ready when Will reached the kitchen from the weaving room where he slept. He ate one bowlful, then took another. His mother and Ann were flurrying about in new lace-edged caps and kirtles. For Will, Mrs. Carey had laid out long woolen hose, carefully mended, clean leather breeches, and a homespun linen shirt.

Mr. Carey had on his best trousers, the ones with shiny buckles below the knee. His long-tailed braided coat was tailor-made from cloth that he himself had woven. He

18

had owned it as long as Will could remember, but used it only for church and holidays. Recently Mr. Carey had spoken often about getting a wig, maybe in time for this Easter. However, the pounds and shillings had not been found for such luxury and, as usual, his rather thin brown hair was neatly brought into a club knot at the nape of his neck and tied with a velvet ribbon.

"Look at me, Will," insisted Ann. In her long dress and winged cap, she looked, Will thought, like a doll-sized model of her mother.

"Everyone ready? We must be in our pew before the bells stop ringing," Mr. Carey reminded the family.

All families of the parish were heading for the village church. They liked to go on Easter, and they had to attend whether they liked to or not, for to be absent without good cause meant a fine of sixpence. In Paulerspury the Church of England directed the lives of the villagers. The parson and the squire, who owned most of the land nearby, were the two most important persons for miles around. Most of the village people were a little bit afraid of them.

As he went inside, Will was proud, as Old Dick had said he would be, to see the flowers he had helped to place on the altar. After his father closed the door to their pew, he could see nothing more on his level. Up high the choir boys were ready to sing, and the parson rose to read the Easter lessons from Mark and John.

Mrs. Carey had taught Will some of the responses which

the congregation was supposed to say at certain times. When at last it was proper to chime in "As it was in the beginning, is now, and ever shall be, world without end, amen," he raised his voice loud and strong above all the others. He thought his father would be proud that he could say the words from memory, but Mr. Carey frowned and nudged him until he squirmed.

Sure enough, after service most people wandered into the close, to look at graves. Mr. Carey stood with bowed head beside the modest headstones of his father and mother and brother William. Will was a little bit sad when he said, "There are dead leaves and trash under the ivy," for he and Old Dick had done the best they could to get around.

"I'll come tomorrow, Fa', and clean beneath it," he offered, and he caught his mother's quick glance of approval.

"Me, too," came from little Ann.

Back home, because it was the sabbath, there was a strange quiet, with no sound of the loom. Parents and children took off their best clothes and put on weekday garb. Will looked forward to dinner. Two fat pheasants were greased and ready for the fireplace spit. He watched his mother push a long iron rod through each bird and stir up the fire.

"Here, Will. Turn them as they brown." This was a job Will liked, but it did not come often. His father had no time to hunt. The pheasants were an Easter gift from the squire. On holidays he sent game to each family in Paulerspury. At Christmas the gift was venison; on May day, lamb.

"Mummy, did you save the pretty feathers?" asked Ann.

"Of course I did. Why? Want to play Indian?"

Will put three fingers to his head and whooped. Mrs. Carey kept talking. "I've heard that an Indian princess named Pocahontas came all the way to London to see our queen, long ago."

"Did she wear feathers like these and a blanket?" asked Will.

Mrs. Carey did not know and she answered vaguely. Getting dinner suddenly claimed her whole attention. She handed Will a drip pan to put under the pheasants, for golden juice was beginning to sputter, and it would make good sopping gravy.

"Stir the embers, Will, and ease this griddle to where it'll find the heat," she directed, motioning to a heavy round of iron mounted on three short legs. "I'm about to stir up corn cakes to bake. It won't take them long."

It didn't. Presently the Careys were around their trestle table, facing the Easter feast. Wooden trenchers, polished clean, served as plates, and each person had a private pewter mug, left by Grandmother Ann who had lived with them until her death a few years back. For the grown-ups, there was ale; for Will and Ann, cambric tea, made from boiling water with a spot of milk and sugar.

Bowing his head, Mr. Carey thanked God rapidly for the bounty of the day. Then he raised his head and said solemnly, "God bless the squire. God save His Majesty, King George."

"God bless the squire. God save His Majesty, King George," repeated the others, sipping their drinks.

Will ate awhile, then remarked, "Willie Hinde told me a funny grace his fa' said one Sunday."

"Tell it," demanded Ann.

"He said:

> 'God bless us as He's able
> And keep us all alive.
> There're ten of us at table
> And food for only five.' "

Mr. Carey scowled. "Not amusing, William. Thanks to the squire, no doubt their rations are enough to go around today, but food is often short for the Hindes. Farming's not the living it was, and the children are too young to be much help. Willie ought to stay more around the place."

"He's going to be bound out, Fa', and learn to be a swineherd, soon's he's ten. He likes pigs."

"So do you, Will," put in Ann. "Why don't you get bound out with him?"

"If I had to be bound out, I'd rather learn to be a gardener, like Old Dick," her brother replied.

"Will will be a weaver. Let's hear no more of it," said Mr. Carey. Will felt a stone in his heart.

The Careys ate in silence for a while, then Will said, "The squire knows me by name."

"How do you know?" asked his father quickly.

"I saw him outside the alehouse Thursday. He said, 'Ho, there, Will Carey, can you read yet?' " Will puffed out his cheeks like the squire's. "And when I said, 'No, sir,' he asked me something else. He asked if my father read his books by candlelight the way he used to."

"What did you say then?" The question came from both parents.

"I told him Fa' was so tired that he went to bed soon's he finished weaving and we had our evening tea."

A troubled look crossed Mr. Carey's face. "We plan you shall learn to read, Will," he said. "But schooling costs money—you know that—and we've none to spare."

"If we had money, it wouldn't do any good," said Will cheerfully. "The school doesn't have a master now."

"Some way will be found," said Mrs. Carey. "A boy with a mind as quick as yours, Will, must have a chance to learn. I wish I could read, so I could teach you."

Will felt pity for his mother, for he knew it was a sorrow to her that she had never been taught to read and write.

By early afternoon the weather, which had been kind all day, turned nasty, with a cold rain and heavy clouds. Mrs. Carey lit candles and a bright block of light shone from the cottage window.

"Please read aloud to us, Fa'. I like it so," urged Will.

Agreeably, Mr. Carey went to the cupboard shelf and brought out his Bible. Will and Ann sat on low stools by the fire as they listened to the story of a boy named David who tended sheep and played a harp and had a friend named Jonathan. To himself, Will became David. He decided to go tomorrow to the meadow, where sheep grazed, to see if there were new lambs. Oh—he had promised to clean out the ivy. Well, he would do that first, then search for lambs.

When the story of David was over, Will begged for more, but Mr. Carey firmly closed the Bible.

"I'll put it in the cupboard, Fa'," Will offered. He handled it with gentle care, and traced out the letters H-O-L-Y B-I-B-L-E with his fingertip. *If I could read,* he thought, *I'd go through every page of this book. I'd find out what happened to David after he became a king. I'd—*

Someone was beating on the door and calling "Edmund Carey! Edmund Carey!" Will jumped to unlatch the bolt. Standing in the rain, but framed by candlelight, was a tallish man carrying a seabag. He wore a wet tan cape, and a three-cornered hat which drooled water. In an instant he had thrown his arms around Will's fa' and was almost sobbing, "Brother! Brother!"

Everyone was happily confused. Questions were tossed like leaves in the wind. Staring open-mouthed, Will tried to take in the fact that this stranger was Uncle Peter, home from Canada after twenty years away. Will had heard

little of his uncle, for no letters had come from him in all those years, and none had gone to him from his family. Uncle Peter, it seemed, had not even known about the birth of Will and Ann—or the death of his mother.

Will longed to ask questions about that faraway place named Canada. He had never even seen a person who had been to a far-off land. Uncle Peter said that he had been on his way three months, sailing over the Atlantic Ocean. Will wanted to ask questions about the ship and the ocean.

Mrs. Carey began to butter leftover corn cakes for her brother-in-law, and swung the iron arm which held the teakettle nearer the fire. Then she put a cake onto a fork and held it before the flame. "This is called 'toast,' Peter, something new since you went away."

"Never had anything so good," he assured her when he had sampled it. "Cakes, made from English corn. Butter from an English cow."

"But the tea comes from India," said his brother.

"We'll forget that. I'm home."

"Uncle Peter, are you going to stay with us?" Will had to ask the question.

"Oh, no, lad. I stopped down at the Three Ravens, when I got off the stage from Liverpool, and told the inn-keeper to hold me a room."

Mr. Carey put an end to that plan. "No public place for my brother," he said. "Not so long as I've a roof over my head."

This pleased Will. He liked the new uncle. "You may sleep on my cot in the weaving room. I'll roll up down here by the fire, if Mummy'll let me."

She did.

The floor was hard before morning, even with two quilts in which Will felt like a cocoon. He awoke with the thought of going to clean out the ivy before breakfast, but rain was beating on the thatched roof. Soon Uncle Peter came down the steps and, without moving, Will watched him. This man was very much like his fa'. He was heavier, taller, more wind- and sun-wrinkled. His hair was thicker, with more gray in it. But his eyes were like Fa's and his own, wide-set and hazel-brown under level brows. Will decided that the Carey men had a way of looking alike, and he was glad.

As Uncle Peter stirred up the fire, Will spoke, "Mummy isn't up yet. It's early."

"That I know. I've been a farmer for twenty years, living alone and eating 'bout dawn. Here, boy, show me where things are and I'll make breakfast."

"No you won't, Peter Carey." Will's mother sailed into the room, white cap in place, tying her apron strings. With a swish of her hand she brushed her brother-in-law from the hearth and took her place as mistress of the kitchen. Easily she put the porridge pot onto its trivet, fetched dried herring from the cupboard, and began to mix batter for more corn cakes. Will's eyes got bigger and bigger. Usually they had one of these things, never all.

"Get the griddle, Will. And the mugs and trenchers."

At breakfast Uncle Peter ate cakes and ate cakes. "I was summat sick on the sea, and sick of the sea. Ships' biscuits got a mite weevilly. I'm making up for three weeks," he explained. Then he asked Mrs. Carey, "Elizabeth, have you any dark sugar?"

"A bit."

"Let's melt it to go over these corn cakes. You'll be surprised how good it is. A French Canadian taught me that."

"We never do—" Ann began, but her father put a finger to his lips.

Flushing with surprise, Mrs. Carey turned to the cupboard. All the family sugar for a month was in a small brown crock, but she poured it onto a saucepan and set it near the fire. In minutes it was gone.

Fa' went upstairs to weave, Mother and Ann to wind yarn. Rain was pouring in what Uncle Peter called "typical English spring weather," but he said it with a smile, as if he felt glad to see it. Will drew up a stool close to Uncle Peter. "Tell me about wild Indians, Uncle Peter," he began.

"They're not wild at all, Will, and not red. Often they speak a kind of French language, which I have learned to understand."

"Why didn't you stay, if you had Indian friends, and a whole farm?"

"It just wasn't England, boy. The miles were too wide, the winters too cold, the sheep too many. All at once I decided to sell out and come home. Maybe I got lonely for the sight of English daisies on a hillside."

"But—but—"

"What 'but?' "

"But I'd like to go to a strange new country, across a sea. I'd like to see Indians in America and Indians in India."

"Perhaps you will, someday. There's plenty of time."

Someday seemed a long time away to Will—as faraway as never.

At two, the mote bell rang, a signal for all men of Paulerspury parish to meet at the church. Every year, on Easter Monday they divided up the work which the whole village shared. Watling Street, the long road running from west to east across England, was always so full of holes after winter that the stage drivers sometimes lost their wheels. The holes near Paulerspury had to be filled. Certain sheep belonged to the church, others to individual families, but all of them grazed in the glebe meadow, and people took turns at being shepherd. This year, the church needed repairs, for the parson said rain came through the thatched roof. Will hated to see his father and uncle start out, but he always looked forward to what his fa' said afterwards. He would be glad when he was old enough to take a turn at sheep herding. It would be fun, with Willie Hinde.

When the men came home, the rain had stopped. Both of them looked serious. Mr. Carey said something to his wife, then she told Will and Ann to go out into the garden for a few minutes. After awhile she called them in. "Your fa' has something to tell you," she said. "Sit you down, both."

Will searched his parents' faces. Had he done something wrong? Tree-climbing? But no, that was two days ago.

Fa' relieved him. "Will, Ann, something important happened to us all this afternoon. The squire asked me to be the village schoolmaster, as my father was. Your mother and I have talked about it, and we agree that I should accept. Among other things, it means that we will not live in this cottage any more, but will move to the empty schoolhouse on the hill."

"You won't weave, Fa'?" The loom had always been part of Carey life, its thrum giving melody and accent to their days; Will could not imagine life without it. Then a bigger thought came. If his father became schoolmaster, perhaps he could go to school and really learn to read.

Mr. Carey was ahead of him. Usually he did not caress his children, but now he took Will's hand. "It means you can go to school, Will. There are several free places in the school. The squire said you might have one of those places."

"This very year?"

"This very year. We'll move at the end of summer, and after that you'll be a schoolboy."

"I'll learn to read!"

"And I feared that day would never come," said Mrs. Carey, softly.

Will was so happy, he could hardly believe any of it.

3
New Home in a Schoolhouse

"Think you can walk all the way to Whittlebury Forest today, Will?" asked Uncle Peter on the first warm morning after his arrival.

The answer was an immediate yes.

"Me, too?" begged Ann.

"Not this time, little lady. I'm not even quite sure Will's legs are long enough to keep up with me. It's a far piece. But somehow I want to smell the English woods."

True, Will's legs were short, but he skipped along well ahead of Uncle Peter. He knew the paths that cows and the sheep had made through farms along the way, and just where to find stiles across stone fences. At some borders there were thick hedges of hawthorn and yew separating the fields; Will had an easier time slithering through these than did the man. Soon their boots were crusty with mud, and they stopped atop a stile to scrape it off.

"You should see the horses jump these fences, Uncle Peter, when there is a fox hunt. The riders wear pink coats, and it's a fine sight. I watch when I can. There's a hunting horn to call the dogs. I want to learn to blow one."

"They'd have a muddy run today, wouldn't they?"

They kept working at their boots, then Uncle Peter said softly, "Listen, Will, a pheasant is crowing."

"Then the birch leaves must be poking out. Willie Hinde's fa' says pheasants crow when the birch trees signal, and it's a sure sign of spring."

Uncle Peter motioned to the slender willows by a little stream which hugged the fence. "Another sign, boy, the willow turning from yellowish gold to silver with that promise of green. I'm feasting my eyes."

"Violets, too, in the moss. Mum loves them, but I guess they'd wilt if I picked some now."

"Up, up and away," challenged Uncle Peter, rising.

"Up, up and away," echoed Will, as he jumped lightly to the ground from the top of the stile.

Whittlebury Forest was a park which belonged to the squire. At certain times people of the parish were permitted to hunt in it, taking deer with bows and arrows, but this was not the season. Will was glad that he would not need to watch for an arrow whizzing through the dappled shadows, but he did hope to see a doe with her fawn, or the huge buck who was said to have tall, tall antlers and could run like the wind. A slight crackle among the twigs made him jump, and he saw a dark purplish groundbird speed away.

"Watch y' ear, Uncle Peter. There's jackdaws about," he warned.

Uncle Peter laughed. He had evidently forgotten that old English joke. Jackdaws were silly birds that liked to take a nip at a visiting ankle in the woods. If a person rested or slept, a nip could come at the ear as well. Some claimed that these birds were so fast they could run up a leg or an arm while one looked for them in the grass.

Deeper in the forest, giant oaks had their new leaves still furled into tight red buds, and below them was a crunchy carpet of acorns, fallen in winter storms. A finch began to sing. Will and his uncle stood without stirring, listening raptly. There was another beautiful sound.

"Wood thrush," whispered Uncle Peter.

A blackbird whistled. Will imitated him perfectly, proud of himself.

"Ssshhhh . . ."

Above them all rose the song of a lark, light, gay, and joyful. They watched him soar into the sky.

Past midday Will's legs became very tired, but he did not dare to say so. Now Uncle Peter was quiet, thoughtful. Will stopped leading, and followed. Finally the man sat down on a grounded log, took a knife from his breeches pocket, and began to whittle a stick.

"What's that, Uncle Peter?"

"Nothing, really. Just remembering. I used to come here and whittle when I was a boy, figuring out what I would do when I became a man. I think I made up my mind in this forest to go to Canada."

"Are you sorry you went?"

"Not one bit. It was a hearty life, though lonely. I learned to make my way, and some guineas besides. But now I'm choosing to stay in this parish the rest of my life. I did think about going to Yorkshire and raising sheep on the downs, but no, I'm going to the squire and rent me a piece of land to farm, and do it."

"When?"

"Soon's I've helped on the Watling Street repairs next month. It was your fa's turn, and I said I'd take his place."

"Uncle Peter, will you teach me how to plant seeds and grow things? I don't want to weave tammy cloth when I grow up, and never get out-of-doors. I like to work in the dirt, and help things grow."

Smiling, Uncle Peter shook Will's hand, man fashion. "I've noticed, Will. You'll be my first assistant farmer. It's a promise."

As the weeks went on, Will was caught up in the business of the family change. Uncle Peter and he went to examine the schoolhouse garden, found it unused for over a year, and full of weeds.

"What say we clear it, Will? Make it ready for your mother's flowers, and plant some things ourselves?"

"What about your farm, Uncle Peter?"

"That can wait. I had no family to help in Canada."

This idea was certainly welcome to Mrs. Carey. Will's fa' kept on with his weaving, for money had to come from somewhere until school began. Every evening, when Uncle Peter and the weary boy came home from the hill, they found a large meal waiting. Since the morning when he had eaten all the sugar, Unce Peter had made ways to add to the food. He caught catfish, trout, and long-legged frogs, then fried them himself on the griddle. Sometimes he snared a rabbit, which he called a 'coney'—Will thought that was a funny word—for the stewpot.

One sundown after they had trimmed and pulled and dug all day, Uncle Peter said to Will, "I've a mind to go to the river for a wash. Can you pick up summat for me at the Three Ravens?"

"Yes, sir. What is it?"

"A surprise for your mother. Tell the innkeeper it's what the stage dropped off for me from Dover. Or was supposed to. Careful, now."

Instead of a box, at the tavern, Will was handed a tightly stitched skinful of water, with a rope sling for carrying. Inside it, something lurched, and Will drew back.

Phil Hoyte, the innkeeper, put him at ease. "It's two fish, lad, Dover sole, and powerful good eatin'. Yer uncle saw some being set down here last week for my tavern table, and ordered some for you Careys. Now look, this here bag is full of sea water. That keeps the fish fresh while they travel from the ocean to the hearth. Think ye can make it home before ye satisfy yer curiosity?"

"First, I've got to figure out how to hold it. I'm sure glad I know it's fish, or I'd be scared."

"You fetch that bag back, or Peter'll have to pay extry for it. I'll pass it on to the driver when he goes back east from Liverpool."

"Yes, sir. Uncle Peter said it was a surprise for Mummy. I can't wait to see her open it."

At home Will asked for the seawater, so Mrs. Carey drained it into a pannikin. He and Ann smelled it deeply. Then Will tasted it. Salty, yes, like people said. But this water wasn't blue like the sea Will had heard about, just dirty and gray, and not at all delicious. Could it ever have been a part of a great plunging wave, in the real ocean? Would he ever see the wide and open sea that Uncle Peter described so often?

That summer never really got very warm, but August came, as usual. Into the Carey family was born another little girl, whom they named Mary.

"Her hands look like little flowers, Mummy," Will declared on his first sight of her.

"Or stars," said their mother.

Mary was something special to come home to, but the cottage was home only a while longer. Moving day, so often talked about, dawned. Men and sturdy boys from other Paulerspury families came to help. Naturally Willie Hinde joined Will.

"You boys move the cooking things," said Mr. Carey, and they set about this special task vigorously. Kettle and stewpots, spit and griddle, trivets and saucepans were carefully transferred to the schoolhouse hearth. Then Will tested the heavy little iron oven that his mother used for baking his favorite rye-and-barley bread. It had a top which fitted tightly, and three stubby legs.

"I guess we'll have to carry this together," he told Willie, "and not try anything else when we do. I sure didn't know an oven could be such a load."

"Bigger'n a pig," agreed Willie.

On their return to the cottage from this delivery, they found Old Dick's pony cart near the gate. The squire had sent it, a neighbor said. Uncle Peter was piling stools and settles and bedding and trenchers and whatever as high as the cart's sides would hold.

He called Will. "Here, boy, just in time. You hop up there now, steady on, and prepare to hold yer mum's spinning wheel so's it won't topple."

Will did that. Old Dick drove the pony; Uncle Peter walked beside the cart. They led a sort of parade down the hollow, with everyone carrying something, past the tree-shaded rectory where the parson lived, and up a grassy incline to their new front door.

There was room for everything, and to spare, for the

schoolhouse had been built, years ago, for a master who had many children of his own.

Mrs. Carey, holding baby Mary in her arms, gave directions, while her husband and brother-in-law and friends carried them out. Will was surprised when she said, "That's Will's bed. Put it in the south bedroom; he's to have that."

"All by my lone, Mummy?"

"It's fitten, Son. You've slept in the weaving room all along, and lately on the floor. I allow you're big enough to have your own place, if we can give it to you. Now we can."

Will saw his parents smile at each other over his head, and knew deep inside their approval of him as a son. He meant to say thank you but somehow he could not speak. *I'll have a place to keep my window plants—and my rocks and butterflies and snakes and frogs.* Will did not voice those thoughts, for he was not sure of his mother's approval. Little by little, though, he intended to turn his room into a garden-zoo.

At bedtime Will lit a candle in his own room, and felt like a squire. From his window he could see the moonlight brightening the water in the moat which separated his family's garden from the parson's lawn. Lily pads made dark round splotches on its shining surface.

As he crawled into bed, the laced ropes gave just a little under the mattress, and he stretched comfortably. Better than the floor, he thought. A bullfrog croaked, then there was a splash into the moat.

I'll find him tomorrow. And I'll get me some tadpoles— then Will was asleep.

4
"Columbus" Carey

Will helped his father clean up the "schoolhouse" part of their new home. It was a separate little room with its own thatched roof, two casement windows, and seats made from rough tree planks. Hot water and scrub brushes, plus a strong dose of pig's-fat-and-lye soap took away the smell of must and mice which had come from long emptiness. After Mr. Carey brought in a narrow wooden table which would serve as his desk, and fitted a shelf to the wall for his few books, all was ready to receive the new batch of scholars.

"What are you going to teach us, Fa'?" asked Will, curiously.

"First, to read and write and cipher. I doubt if many get farther than that this year."

"Where am I going to sit?"

"We'll see how many come. You'll probably be the smallest, and sit up front."

"I told Mummy I'd try hard to be good, Fa'."

"You'll be that, all right. There'll be no trouble from the master's son, I'll tell you now."

Will shivered a little at the new sharp tone in his father's voice.

"And, Will . . ."

"Yes, sir?"

"No more calling me 'Fa'.' It's well enough in a cottage, but from now on, we're in public life. Remember to say 'Father,' or better still, in the schoolroom just 'Sir.' "

"Oh."

"One more thing. This is Monday. Wednesday afternoon at five, before vespers, report to the church for the boys' choir. I'm parish clerk now, as well as schoolmaster, and you should be singing with the others. The parson spoke to me about it."

"Yes, Fa'. I mean 'Sir.' " Singing in the choir! What would that mean? He didn't know all those psalms and chants, but he supposed he could learn. For a moment he was flooded with longing for the cottage and the familiar thump-thump of the loom, for mornings roaming with Willie Hinde or following Old Dick about the squire's pretty garden.

Ann appeared at the schoolhouse door, and bade them both come outside at once. Then, unable to keep her little secret, she burst out "Pigs!"

She was right. The squire's pigman stood at their scullery door, escorting a strange gift, a mother sow with five baby piglets. "For you, Mr. Carey," he said, touching his forehead in a sort of salute, "from the squire himself, with his compliments. There's an old pen back here some-place; I'll just herd them inside, but you'd better mind the gate, 'coz she may decide to go home."

Thanks were said, and the visitor was offered a cup of hot tea to cool him off after his higgledy-piggledy walk down the lane. The journey had made the piglets thirsty, too, so the sow lay on her side to refresh them while Will and Ann stared in delight.

"Wait 'till I tell Uncle Peter. He'll be that glad!" exclaimed Will.

Things were different now that Uncle Peter was not around all the time. He had chosen to remain in the old Carey cottage, alone, except for the evening meals which he had been invited to share every day.

"There's another good thing, Edmund," Mrs. Carey told her husband.

"Yes?"

"The parson's wife came to call. She brought a bowl of clotted cream and six beautiful ripe peaches, and she says that their cow has a new calf so they have lots and lots of milk. She wants us to send Will over late every afternoon with a pannikin. As long as they have milk to spare, she will give it to us. With our baby so tiny, I'll be right glad to get it. I must make her some lace, soon's I can find the time. I never dreamed the gentry would be all this kind."

"We've come up summat in the world, Elizabeth. Take what life offers, the better with the bitter. I just hope I can do what's expected of me. I'm a good weaver, but I shall have to work very hard not to be a poor schoolmaster."

"Don't be afeard, Edmund. Who reads aloud more clearly? Or writes a firmer hand? Not the squire. I've heard him read the lessons at evensong. And I daresay, not the parson either."

Mr. Carey admired the squealing piglets, while their fat mother huffed and snorted. Then he told his wife, "I could do with some fresh pork. With five, we could spare one. Wonder if Peter knows how to butcher?"

Will paled. Fa'—no 'Father'—was planning to kill a baby pig, right off. Upset, he ran toward the village to get comfort from his uncle. By the time he reached the cottage, though, he knew that he must learn not to mind. He himself liked sausage, or a puckering pickled pig's trotter, and roast pork of a Sunday was fit for King George himself.

Uncle Peter sympathized, but pointed out to Will that it was the same with lambs, squirrels, any kind of meat. "You can't be too tied up with farm beasts, laddie. Your heart'll break often if you do."

"It's—well, we haven't had any of our own before."

"I know. I was a boy m'self before I was a man. Book learning is hard, but life learning is harder."

Within a few days Will could agree to that, for he had his first taste of book learning. The first morning the school bell rang, twenty scholars came to enrol. As his father had predicted, he was the youngest and the shortest of them all, and he was given a front seat. Fa' seemed like a stranger, behind his desk, and it proved easy enough to call him 'Sir,' as the other boys did.

The Bible was Mr. Carey's main textbook. Over and over he and his pupils repeated simple verses from the holy Book. Then he taught them to read the words, later to find them in the Bible, at last to copy them. When Will could recognize a few words without help, he was happy. "I can read!" he boasted to Ann, then proved it.

Writing, practiced with a goose quill, was more difficult. "Sir" insisted that all letters be made small and neat. To study numbers, the pupils had acorns and sticks. If "Sir" put eight acorns on his desk and took five away, three were left. Everybody knew that, thought Will. Day after day, week after week, month after month the same thing went on. All it took to get good marks was a quick memory. Will's active mind grew restless.

Recess was welcome to them all. "Sir" gave the word and all twenty students tried to get out the door at the same time.

There was a game called "Stagastagaroney," which the boys played every day. One person was "It." He chased all until he had a captive, then the captive was bound to capture another, and so on until everyone was captured at last.

Will's legs, though short, were fast. For kickball, where sides were chosen, he was always wanted. And he liked to wrestle on the grass.

Of course on Wednesdays now he obeyed his father and went to practice with the choir. No longer did he sit with his parents and sisters at services; he sang with the other boys in the loft. They wore waist-length robes and flowing black ties. With their Sunday-scrubbed faces, they seemed very handsome to Ann, and she wished little girls could sing in church.

Some days "Sir" would tell a story. One morning he told of an adventurous sailor named Christopher Columbus, who would not take no for an answer when he wished to make a dangerous voyage. Believing that the world was round, though others were certain it was flat, he sailed away and found a whole new land, known now as America.

When Will learned that Columbus was also the son of a weaver, his excitement grew, and he talked so much about Columbus that his schoolmates began to call him that. At Stagastagaroney, when he was caught, someone would shout "I've got Columbus!" Though the big boys laughed, Will rather liked it. Columbus had dared to strike out for an unknown land. He had felt the beckoning of faraway places, as Will so often did. There was no harm or shame in being thought adventuresome.

5
Roses, Bugs—and Sneezes

"Rise."
The boys rose.
"Sing."
The boys sang.

> God bless our noble King.
> God save Great George, our King.
> God save the King.

School was out for another day. Will slipped through the door and made tracks for the village. Late every afternoon, now, a group of men gathered at Three Ravens to ring handbells. It was a serious sport, watched by silent but enthusiastic spectators. Will stood as near the ringers as he dared, not to be in the way.

There were eight bells in the set owned by citizens of Paulerspury parish. Each bell varied a tiny bit in thickness from the other, so that when they were rung, they gave a different tone. Small leather handles were riveted to the metal cups. When not in play, the bells were placed carefully upon a table covered with a thick cloth; this way they could become perfectly still. When the leader nodded, each man would pick up his bell by the handle, steady it in his hand, and be ready to ring it at the perfect, proper moment.

Propped up on the table was a diagram of the order in which the bells were to be rung. The men called this diagram a "pattern," and followed it closely. Will knew that his mother used a pattern for her lace-making, but he was surprised that there was one for bell-ringing, too.

The tunes that the men rang were called "changes." These changes had special names. There was "Kent," which was not particularly appealing to Will. But other changes, such as "grandsire triples," "treble bob major," and "treble bob royal" won cheers from him and the older crowd.

During a practice change, Will squatted to see exactly what each man did. As his turn came, the ringer would swing his bell for a complete circle, and rest it bottom up at the end of the swing. Wrist and eye had to work together because the little clapper had to strike the metal at precisely the right time to make a true note for the playing of the pattern.

After a grand flourish of "grandsire triples" the leader called a rest, and ordered cider for his men. Will joined others who filed by the table to look at the bells that could make such beautiful sounds.

"Like them, Will Carey?" asked Mr. Tom Pluckett, a friend of his father's.

"Oh, yes, sir. I do. I'd sure be pleased to touch one."

"Well, touch this one; it's as good as mine. I put in a guinea to help buy the set."

"Why eight, Mr. Tom?"

"That's all this village could pay for. Eight's enough really. With eight bells you can ring 40,000 changes. Think of that."

"How long would it take?"

"How's your arithmetic?"

"Father says it's improving over last year."

"Well, Will, I'll tell you that 20,000 changes would take twelve hours, steady. Now how long would 40,000 take?"

Will wrinkled his forehead, then answered: "Twenty-four hours, Mr. Tom."

"You're right! How old are you now, boy?"

"Nine, going on ten."

"You figure well in your mind for nine. Now here's another one. Bells are rung at two strokes a second. How many strokes in twenty-four hours?"

"I give up."

"So do I," Mr. Tom laughed.

Then he told Will, while others surrounded them to listen, that bell-ringing was popular all over England, and in Belgium, too, he'd heard. And it was said that with twelve bells, so many changes could be rung that it would take ninety-one years to ring them all.

"Too much arithmetic, Mr. Tom. I'm not really very good at it. I'd rather just listen. That is, if I can't learn to play."

"You can, when you're older. Bell-ringing is a man's business. If our group gets expert enough we're going to enter the contest over at Piddington next market day."

"Time, gentlemen, time," called Phil Hoyte. "Back to the bell table. Try 'treble bob major' again. The pattern's all set and ready."

It was dark before Will left the tavern. He rushed to the rectory for the evening pail of milk, and saw with relief that his father was in the parson's drawing room, deep in conversation. His mother, he knew, would not scold him for being late.

At home, he put down the milk, lifted Mary over his head until she squealed for him to stop, then he carried her gently to the cradle in their mother's room where baby Thomas lay. Thomas cooed and gurgled, pleased with attention. Already he thrust his arms and legs from under the covers, showing more action and vigor than Mary ever had.

Something was the matter with Mary's back; nobody said what. Anyway, at nearly three she was not able to walk alone. When he was at home, Will carried her, usually on his shoulders, wherever she wanted to go.

Nothing was the matter with Mary's voice. She talked plainly, and now she was old enough to ask for what she needed, so she did not have to cry as she had when she was younger. Will knew that she adored him.

Paulerspury schoolboys called their vacation "summer hols." This summer Will spent his free time in the garden. His mother gave him a plot of his own. In it he planted pinks and bluebells and anemones and bleeding hearts.

Old Dick offered fine bulbs—tulips and lilies from the manor house. But he gave Will something more valuable. He shared with him his own wisdom about plants and their ways—a wisdom he had been storing up over a long lifetime. "It takes more than knowledge—something up here—to grow fine flowers," Old Dick tapped his forehead. "You have to have a feeling for growing things—to understand how they feel."

Will seemed to have that feeling—to know what his flowers needed and wanted. All of Paulerspury talked about the way things grew for him.

Will roamed the fields and woods to find out all he could about wild plants. He studied birds, watching them at their nest-making and listening to their calls. His room at home was so full of potted plants, grasses, weeds, discarded birds' nests, butterflies, snails, and such that the family began calling it the garden-zoo.

Most days as he worked in his garden, Will took Mary

with her blanket and placed her on the footpath. Giving her a little fork, he gravely asked her "help" in softening the dirt. By late afternoons, though, he carried her indoors and ran for the village green. There, the village boys played football.

Will was short but he could outrun almost anybody, and when the ball bounced on his head, he discovered that he had a "tough noggin." When sides were chosen, quite soon a captain said, "I'll tek Will Carey."

Warm weather brought thousands of little bugs to Mrs. Carey's roses. One morning at breakfast she asked the children to pick them off. They liked this task.

"Take me," chimed in Mary.

"Remember, Ann, how you used to say that all the time?"

Ann shrugged. She was usually busy about girl-things now. Her mother had taught her to make lace, to spin, and to cook simple meals. This summer she had pared lots and lots of apples and peaches, and set them out on boards to dry, for winter eating. However, she still had fun with Will, whenever he noticed her, and she loved to garden.

Picking off bugs and drowning them in a pannikin of water was a game. They counted aloud, to see who got the most. Mary parroted the numbers as they said them. Will sneezed. Mary mimicked that, too. He sneezed again, with a loud "Ah-chooooo!"

"God bless you," said Ann.

"Thank you. Ah, ah, ah–choo!"

"You look all puffy and red, something like Willie Hinde," Ann told him.

"I feel funny. I itch. I've itched most of this summer," Will confessed.

"And sneezed," Ann added. "I guess I've said 'bless you' ten thousand times." She looked curiously at Will. "You know, the minute you plant something or work around Mummy's roses, you turn all red and sneezy."

"Don't say that. First place, 'tisn't so. Next place, I'm going to be a farmer, and I'll have to work in the dirt. I just catch cold, summers."

"Suit yourself, smarty."

"Ah, ah–a-chooo!"

"Bless you."

"Thank you."

When Mrs. Carey saw Will's red, splotchy face, she went straightaway to put the copper on to boil, and said he should take an allover bath.

"Why, Mum? It's not Saturday or anything."

"It'll make you more comfortable. And you're to rest in bed awhile. Here, Peter brought up this newspaper last night, after the stage came through. You look at it until your father wants it."

With this pleasure ahead, Will bathed meekly, and the itching seemed better. The newspaper, the *Mercury,* was the only one published in Northamptonshire, and but three copies came to Paulerspury. The squire paid for them all—one for himself, one for the parson, and one for the schoolmaster. There was one issue a week.

Since Will had learned to read, he had been devoted to the *Mercury*. From it he learned what was going on beyond Paulerspury, which towns had market fairs, whose pigs took prizes for being the fattest, what days sheep should be taken to the shearers. Sometimes he read about the King. In letters to the paper, men often called him "Farmer George." Other writers said he was a German who could not even speak the English language well. Whatever was printed was of interest to Will. He read and read. As he read he scratched and sneezed, but he only knew that he was reading.

"Oh, Will! It's time to get the milk," called Ann.

"Already?"

"You've been in there all afternoon. I've been out and picked gooseberries and made a lovely berry fool for our supper. Mummy says to hurry now. Uncle Peter'll be here soon."

With practiced hands Will folded the *Mercury*. His father liked it in exact order. He was glad it was nearly suppertime. Gooseberry fool was his favorite summer pudding, all the way from the sponge cake on the bottom to the clotted cream on top.

"I'll be—ah-choo—right there. Hand me the pail as I come by."

6
A New Kind of Adventure

Oftener than not, after Will reached his first teens, he came home very late in the afternoons from the village. On rainy days he watched the bell ringers, who were getting better all the time, as they mastered a great number of changes. Sometimes he went to the blacksmith's shop, where men and boys gathered to pass the time of day. Football, marbles, wrestling, horseshoe pitching, kite-flying all claimed him. He liked to be with people, and people seemed to like him.

Uncle Peter had found his farm—several miles away but still on the squire's land. When he thought Will was free from school, he asked him to come out and help, but during term time he did not want to disturb the boy's chances of being a scholar. He himself had been to school only a few years, and he was proud that Will seemed bright at books.

However, Will had little need to study his lessons. Year after year his father taught the same things, as his own

56

father had done before him. Already Will could read and write and recite Scripture and reel off his "times tables" through the twelves. Also, he knew about money and how to count it—pounds, shillings, and pence—though he never had any of his own.

Uncle Peter did not come often, but every evening there was a place set at table for him, and when the children heard him whistling up the path, they ran to meet him. His hands were never empty. He might be carrying a basket of eggs covered with fresh brussels sprouts, or a live goose squawking over his shoulder. If he killed a sheep, there was a joint for Sunday, and pieces of mutton for a dish which Mrs. Carey made called "Lancashire hot pot."

The "hot pots" were better after Uncle Peter ordered out some pounds of pepper from London. One winter night, when cold fog seemed to find its way to a person's bones, all mouths were watering, for lamb and potatoes and onions had been sending out a delicious come-hither smell.

"Come, Ann, and watch me add the pepper corns so's you'll know how much, in case you ever have any."

"Why might I not have any, Mum?"

"It's like gold, so dear to buy."

Pepper certainly made a difference in the taste of the hot pot. There was scarcely enough left for dripping on torn bread tomorrow.

"I've a question, Will," said Uncle Peter.

Will was ready.

"Can you say 'Peter Piper picked a peck of pickled pepper?' "

Everybody tried except Mr. Edmund Carey. Mary said it remarkably well, but little Thomas only got as far as "Peter Piper."

"And do you know why Peter Piper picked a peck?" Uncle Peter kept on.

"No, sir."

"Because the pickled meat he had to eat without pepper was so danged awful."

Mr. Carey scowled. "This language is not for the children's ears, Peter."

"Oh, Edmund—" began Mrs. Carey, but that gentleman had risen to leave the kitchen.

"Will," he said, "I want to speak to you in the schoolhouse."

And now what? Will felt that his father was increasingly displeased with him, for some reason, and he was soon to learn why.

"Sit down at your place," ordered Mr. Carey, in his schoolmaster-parish clerk voice.

Of course Will sat.

"Where were you this afternoon?"

"At Three Ravens."

"I thought so. And yesterday?"

"I forget."

"Then I'll remind you. First, at Three Ravens. Then, until dark, at the blacksmith's being smarty about what was in the newspaper. I won't have it, Will. I am a leader in this parish, and I don't like to hear that my son may be found loitering in public places."

"But what's the harm?"

"Enough. You watch your step, young man. As soon as you're old enough, we'll find honest work for you to do. At your age I was earning my keep weaving tammy cloth. Your mother has spoiled you, letting you run so free."

Shocked and hurt, Will tried not to cry. Not go to hear the bell ringers? And who had told his father that he sometimes showed off a little at the blacksmith's? He could read, and big men couldn't. What was the matter with telling them what they wanted to know?

For the first time in his life, Will became really angry with his father, angry all over. He intended to keep on doing these things which he liked so much and which harmed nobody, but guilt and sadness mingled with his sense of unfairness. Never again, he feared, when he heard the thrilling peal of the bells would there be an echo of joy within his own heart.

He went to his room and pressed the door shut. Here, among his own butterflies, rocks, and potted plants, he wiped away the few spilled tears. Then his tingling eyes fell on the tadpole jar. Some of the creatures were beginning to lose their tails. Fascinated, he watched until it was too dark to tell one from another, then he pulled the bed covers over his head and tried to lose himself in sleep.

Fortunately the next day was Saturday. Without stopping for porridge he was out the garden gate, across the moat, and away. Yellow fog still thickened the air. The earth was returning his gloom. Old Dick would welcome him, and he had not been forbidden the manor-house grounds. He found his tanned, wrinkled friend sitting inside the stable, whittling a length of boxwood. A warm smell of beasts and hay soothed Will's troubled spirit, and he was able to say "mornin' " to Old Dick in his usual way.

"And the same to you, lad. Pull up a milking stool and sit you down."

"Making summat?"

"Aye. A flute for my least grandchild."

"Any special kind of wood you're using?"

" 'Tis that. Boxwood. Old *'buxus sempervirens'* itself."

"Old what?"

" *'Buxus sempervirens.'* That's the Latin name for it, my fa' told me. He learned a lot of strange things from the old squire, he did."

"Is that the real name of the green hedge we just call 'box,' *buxus sempervirens?*" Will's tongue twisted around the strange new words, and he said them again, *"buxus sempervirens."*

Old Dick nodded. "So 'tis. All flowers and plants, my fa' told me, have proper names in the Latin language. Maybe in some other tongue, too, I dunno. But he said that long word, *sempervirens,* means 'always green,' and that must be right, for it's green the year round, we both know."

"And *buxus?*"

"Well, it's a fine carving wood, and when it's old enough to be big enough, just right for making boxes. Sounds as if 'box' is just a shortnin' for *buxus.*"

"Has the squire a book that tells all this?"

"Mebbe yes and mebbe no. He's not the bookman his fa' was. And I can't say, ennyhow; I can't read, Will Carey."

"You can do lots of other things, Old Dick. But who could tell me about those Latin names for things?"

Old Dick whittled quietly for a few moments, then said, in a "maybe" sort of voice, "I hear the new weaver, that Thomas Jones fellow, started out to be a doctor and has a passel of education beyond the rest of us."

Here was something new, a language to explore, as one follows a secret path in the woods. Will admired the beginnings of the flute, thanked his friend, and set off for the weaver's cottage in Paulerspury.

It was not the house where he had lived, but the throb of the loom was the same familiar, regular sound he had known all of his childhood. He waited outside the door until Mr. Jones paused for a rest and came to get a breath of air. Hastily, lest he be stopped too soon, Will explained his errand. The weaver, a youngish man with an unhappy face and broody eyes stared at the boy in disbelief.

"Why, yes, I've studied Latin," he admitted, "but I've no idea how to teach it. What is it you want?"

"Just the names of plants, first, please. But later I'd like to know it all."

Thomas Jones threw back his head and laughed. "That's a good one! Nobody ever knows all of anything. I don't even remember what I did know."

"But do you know where to find it?" pressed Will.

"I suppose so."

Thomas must have thought that teaching Latin to this boy would break the tiresomeness of tammy-weaving. He did know Latin, and many other things, Will learned later, because he had been to the famous Kidderminster Grammar School before he tossed over his father's plan for him to become a doctor. This round-faced child with the dimple in his chin looked bright. He was certainly eager. Looking somewhat surprised, the weaver agreed to tutor Will in Latin.

"Come in, Will Carey. We'll make a pot of tea and talk plans."

Though the tea was hot and dark and good, Will forgot to drink as he listened to the young weaver.

"Soon after the time of Jesus Christ, the Romans came

to England," he said. "They brought, of course, their skills and customs and language. Wherever we look, here in England, we see things that they built—old walls, forts, roads. Watling Street, where you walk every day, is a Roman road. And their language, the Latin you want to learn, still seasons our English speech like salt and pepper."

Mr. Jones brought out an exercise book. Will pushed aside his teacup and lifted his eager face for the first instruction.

"A group of words is called a vocabulary. That word is from Latin, too. Write 'vocabulary' at the top of the page." Mr. Jones spelled out the word slowly as Will wrote.

"First words, now. We'll start with *buxus sempervirens,* since that was what brought you here."

Smiling, Will traced out the Latin words, letter by letter. In a short while, he had a list of twenty words.

"Enough this time," said Thomas Jones. "Learn those and come back. We'll have new words every week."

Within a few days Will stood knocking again at the weaver's door. Soon he knew eighty Latin words, then a hundred. Studying them was fun, but it was more than a game. It was accomplishment. As he worked in his garden or walked in the woods, Will practiced calling plants by their Latin names. And he found that knowing those names gave him new understanding of the plants.

7

Not Meant for Farming

Peter Carey stopped in Three Ravens to post a notice that he had pigs for sale. Standing at the public board, where such signs were placed, was his nephew Will, reading aloud an announcement of sports to be held at Piddington, eight miles distant, on Michaelmas Day, September 29, 1773.

There were to be games and prizes and contests a-plenty. As Will read the descriptions of contests, his listeners guffawed and slapped one another on the back. Peter kept out of Will's sight. The boy seemed to be having a good time.

"To be played for a cricket, a round of beef," read Will. "A cheese to be rolled downhill. Prize to whoever stops it. A prize for grinning through horse collars. A Michaelmas goose to be dived for. A handsome hat for the boy most expert in catching a roll dipped in treacle, and suspended by a string. A good hat to be wrestled for. A pig to be given to whoever catches it by the tail. A leg of mutton to the winner of a race of a hundred yards in sacks. Football, cricket, skittles, and rounders on the green."

As Will left the tavern a while later, he met his uncle on the road to the schoolhouse. Wondering whether he had been seen, he flushed and fumbled his greeting. The man did not leave him guessing.

"Quite a list of sports, I'd say. Why don't we go over to Piddington for the holiday? There'll be no school on Michaelmas, I'm sure."

"Oh, Uncle Peter, Father'll find something for me to do here. He gets to thinking all fun's sinful."

"Leave that to me. I've a mind to take some pigs to sell at the marketplace. I can ask you to go along to help me handle them in the pony cart. There'd be no objection to that."

Nor was there. Will spent the night before Michaelmas at the farm, and before dawn they were off in the pony cart, with a crate of squealing porkers. The road was rough and narrow, but all movement seemed to be in the same direction, toward Piddington, and there was a holiday feel in the air. About halfway there they overtook Willie Hinde, afoot, and invited him to ride. He was bound out to the squire now, working with the manorhouse animals and liking it. This meant, though, that he and Will saw each other less often than in former years, so a full day together was a fine prospect.

"What're you going to enter, Will?" he asked.

"I may grin through the horse collar."

"Tell you what, let's race in the sacks."

Uncle Peter laughed. "Will would beat you, Willie Hinde. He's light and quick on his feet. Myself, I'm going to try for the cheese."

It was a gay day. For lunch they ate pasties and tarts, bought by Uncle Peter from the parish ladies at one of their booths. Uncle Peter also bought some crocks of salmon paste for Mrs. Edmund Carey, and a setting of duck's eggs for Ann.

At noon, a square-faced man wearing a hat with a very wide brim announced that contests would begin. The boys joined a crowd of merrymakers, ready to compete.

"In my hands is a nice plump roll tied to a long string," shouted the man. "See, now, I am dipping it in treacle." He shoved the roll all the way down in a bowl of sticky, syrupy jelly. "Whoever catches the roll wins a loverly prize—a hat just like me own. I'm about to throw it— one, two, three."

Men and boys kicked and jumped and grabbed, but Willie Hinde was nearest the end of the string. He made a fist tight around the roll, and gummy stuff ran through his fingers onto his sleeve. Quickly, he began to lick the treacle, his face getting redder and redder.

The man waved his hat high above the crowd, pointed to Willie and asked, "Yer name, lad? And yer village?"

"Willie Hinde, sir. From Paulerspury."

"Here ye be." The man tossed a hat toward him, and he caught it with his left hand. In a second it was on his head, down almost to his nose.

"I never saw you in a hat before," said Will.

"Never had one," mumbled Willie, still eating the roll.

"How'm I going to grin, now, through the horse collar, Uncle Peter?"

"Look at Willie in his big hat, and smile for all you're worth. I believe you'll come out a winner."

"Ready with the horse collar," called the square-faced man. "Grinners, hunt up yer smiles, you're going to need them. You watchers, clap for the one you think the best."

Will got in line. The horse collar was hanging from a tree limb, a little high for him, but he stood on tiptoe when his turn came. Willie winked at him and pulled the big hat farther over his face. Its feather plumes brushed his shoulder. Will broke into his broadest grin—and won the contest.

They stayed until dark fell on the last game of rounders and the players could no longer see the ball. The bumpy ride home seemed quiet without pig noises. Fog settled in drops on their hair. A horned owl turned his head to watch them as they passed his perch on a hawthorn branch.

At Uncle Peter's, Will fell asleep across a mattress made of rushes, and in what seemed but minutes it was morning, with his uncle shaking his shoulder.

"Ladle out yourself some porridge, Will. I've summat to say to you ere you go home. First, there's cold water in the ewer; wash your eyes to shed the sleep. 'Twas a happy day at the fair, was it not?"

"Best ever."

"I thank you for helping me with my pigs, and being company. This night I've done some hard thinking."

"I've done some hard sleeping."

"Well, put on your thinking cap now, and heed what I say."

"Yes, sir."

"I know you like school, but you've gone as far as is taught. There's no use in repeating things you know already. Yer fa's getting restless about you. It's time you learned a trade or found some way to earn a living. Now for some years I've meant to take you in with me, did you wish to come. You've the makings of a good farmer, boy, with your love of the land and its creatures. Your father is agreeable, though he thought for a time you'd learn weaving."

"I'd hate it," said Will. "I want to work outdoors."

"Suppose I ask your father if you could move out here now. It's the fall of the year, to be sure, but there's plenty to be done yet. For one thing, it's my turn to plant the glebe meadow in turnips for the village sheep, and that's a two-man job."

"You mean leave home?"

"In a way. Not as far as I did when I set out for Canada. We can still put our feet under your mum's good table some of the time, if she's willing."

"Do you think I could be one half of a 'two-man job'?"

"That I do, or I wouldna' bring it up."

Together, they presented the plan to Will's parents and it was approved. Mrs. Carey turned aside to shed a tear, but the schoolmaster was glad to have his older son well occupied. Peter promised to pay for Will's services with farm produce, at first, and when they left, the boy carried a change of clothing in a roll strapped upon his back.

Will was thirteen, still short, but strong, and a determined worker. First, his uncle assigned him a job marking his sheep, for come winter they would be turned out into the common meadow to graze. Dipping a stick into a pot of red dye, he made a circle on the wool of the hind thighs. That was the easy part. First he had to catch the sheep, and even in a pen it was something to lay hands on one. From the bellowing that went on, one might think a butchering was taking place. Before he finished, Will had red spots, too.

"Now go to the manor house before night, and ask the loan of an ox for Thursday if the day be fine. I've spoken to the squire about it, but didn't set the time," said Uncle Peter.

"For the glebe meadow? Turnips?"

"Yes, it's time to seed the winter crop, so's there'll be sumpin' green for the sheep to munch. Makes their wool have more gloss, and fattens 'em, too. Better texture to the meat."

"Uncle Peter, why do we say 'glebe meadow'?"

"That means a meadow owned by the Church of England, but used by all of us here in the parish. You see, we pay our tithes at Christmas time to the church, and that gives us a few privileges. We have a parson to marry us and bury us and read the lessons to us on Sunday, and we have the use of the meadows and the streams."

"Oh! I hadn't thought about any of that."

"Well think on't while you do my errand. The Church of England is a big part of our lives, here in this parish. It's not just a stone building with a square tower and bells. I missed it on my sheep farm in Canada, I tell you. When you're older, you'll understand that a man needs his church, and the church needs its men. That's part of God's plan, mebbe. But here, I'm no parson. Off with you."

When the seeds had been sown, Will and his uncle took hoes and covered them lightly with dirt. It was a full day's work. Will's face grew redder and redder, and all through supper he sneezed.

"Took cold, I guess, getting too hot, hoeing," said Uncle Peter. "I'll get you snugged down for the night, soon."

Will did not need urging. His muscles ached, and he was as sleepy as he had ever been in his life. He did not even object when Uncle Peter produced a nightcap, which he called a 'biggin,' and tied it on his head, saying it would keep off draughts.

At home, he had read over his vocabulary lists and memorized a few new Latin words every night. Tonight he did not think about Latin; he was too busy sneezing.

In an hour he was awake, his skin on fire. He itched all over. Weary, he went back to sleep, and woke again. Next morning his eyes felt full of sand and his nose ran.

"Here, I'll make you a hot posset," Uncle Peter offered, and Will drank it down gratefully.

Strong sun and wind of an outdoor life proved not to be Will's friends. Every day spent in the field, at whatever task, meant sneezing and redness of skin. After several months even Uncle Peter began to wonder whether Will would get over this discomfort; whether he could really turn the boy into a farmer. He was willing enough just to let him "help," but someday Will would be a man grown, with no uncle to depend on, and he would have to have the health to manage the long hours of a farmer's life. It was hard to find Will now when he was not scratching, as much as he tried to stop it.

" 'Tis a pity, Edmund, but the lad's not meant for farming," Peter told his brother.

"Then we must make other plans. He's set against

weaving. I'll talk to the squire," said Mr. Carey. Will was mortified and disappointed.

Before the talk with the squire, however, an advertisement in the Northampton *Mercury* changed Will's life. A cobbler, Clarke Nichols of Piddington, put it in the paper that a Paulerspury boy, a certain William Robinson who was apprenticed to him, had run away.

Mr. Carey read aloud to his wife: "He was wearing a blue coat, buff-colored waistcoat, leather breeches joined in the thighs, speckled stockings, and scuttle hat. If he is seen, detain him. Send information to the youth's father, or to me, Clarke Nichols."

"Do you know the lad, Mr. Carey?"

"By sight. I doubt he'll return to Paulerspury, or that Clarke Nichols would have him back. His father will have to forfeit his apprentice fee, a good sum, I daresay."

"Poor lad. How old is he?"

"Seventeen, it says. No 'poor lad' at all. He'd no right to run away, and on a Sunday morning, too."

A thoughtful look shadowed Mr. Carey's face and he remarked, "Elizabeth, this means that there's a place open for an apprentice at the cobbler's. What about our Will?"

8
The Cobbler's Apprentice

Mr. Clarke Nichols accepted fourteen-year-old Will Carey as an apprentice cobbler. For this there was a charge of ten pounds a year, high for a schoolmaster to pay, but Uncle Peter offered to furnish some of it.

An apprentice was expected to spend seven years learning his craft. From absolutely nothing, which was certainly what Will knew about making shoes, an expert cobbler would be trained. If, at twenty-one, he did his work well and paid attention, he would be able to earn a living and support a family, provided he had one. Seven years seemed to Will a long time to look ahead.

One visit a month would be allowed at home. Mary was to have Will's room. When Will had gone to Uncle Peter's farm, he had left most of his treasures behind. Now he gave his window plants to Ann. The bluebird with the mended wing in its handmade cage, he gave to Mary. She liked to talk to the bird, and it was tame enough to eat from her hand.

"But the water-babes, Mary, we'd best pour back into the moat," he decided. They made a special ceremony of doing it. Mary had learned to walk a short distance, if someone was nearby to help. Will felt that he would miss this little sister most of all.

Uncle Peter came to drive Will to Piddington in his pony cart. The eight miles stretched on and on for the heavyhearted boy, so unlike the gay ride on Michaelmas Day.

The hawthorn hedges were in bloom, and Will saw young rabbits scuttling beneath them. *What blooms or runs about in a cobbler's shop?* he wondered gloomily.

"You'll find you make many kinds of shoes, Will. You should see those the Indians wear, the kind they call moccasins. Deerhide can be made very soft, but it is also tough and warm. Sometimes they just cut out pieces bigger than the foot, and tie them tight around their ankles. I've seen some, though, that were very fancy, laced with narrow leather thongs, and decorated with colors got from berry juices."

No answer.

Uncle Peter tried again. "I hear tell there's a kind of shoe worn at court called duckbill, with soles so wide they get in folks' way. Passed a law saying they could not stick out more'n six inches on a side."

Silence.

Peter left the subject of shoes alone, and brought up

something for Will to look forward to. "First time you're
home, Will, we'll have to fix us a badger-set. Have you
seen that big fat granddaddy badger?"

Will nodded that he had, then he stared glumly at a
group of sheep cropping away at a green patch beside the
road. Disturbed, the leader looked up at the cart with
angry yellow eyes. Will knew how he felt.

Piddington was a long narrow village, like Paulerspury,
and Clarke Nichols' home was in the center of things. It
was a well-built house, smaller than the schoolhouse, and
much more cluttered with furniture. Small rugs covered
the floor. A mantel over the fireplace was filled with
figures of china dogs and people. Near a window, on one
wall, was a shelf of books. Will strained to see the titles;
they were little to his taste, all on religious subjects, but
they were print, and he resolved to read them soon.

With Uncle Peter present, Mr. Nichols was the genial
host. It took but a minute for Will to take his clothing to
the attic he was to share with the other apprentice, John
Warr. Then the cobbler hastened them to a long room
which smelled of soaking hides and which he called "our
workshop." John rose from his bench to be introduced,
and returned quickly to his stitching.

"I've provided ye an apron," said Mr. Nichols, as he
held up a leather coverall. "Hmmm, too long. I'd no
idea a fourteen-year-old would be this short. Well, that's
easily remedied. Can't stretch the boy, can cut the apron."

Will felt that he was expected to laugh, but he couldn't. In the next breath Mr. Nichols was finding another fault with him, this time about his hair. All his boyhood his mother had trimmed his wavy hair, first placing a wooden bowl over the top of his head, and cutting around it. For some weeks this had not been done, and the joggly ride to Piddington had shaken his locks considerably.

"When you can hold that hair together, club it at the back," directed Mr. Nichols. "Otherwise it will fall into your eyes as you lean over to work. John here will find you a leather string to tie it."

Next he pointed out the tools, naming them: awls, hammers, scrapers, chisels, drawknives, pincers, a lapstone, rubbing sticks. Will caught John looking at him with sympathy and understanding, and as Mr. Nichols turned for a second to examine the hides in the leather vat, John gave him a friendly wink. Will's heart bounded for the first time that day.

"You and I'll eat at the public house, Mr. Carey," suggested Mr. Nichols. "John's brought in two pork pies, I think, and there's tea. The boys can get acquainted, and be ready for work when I get back."

This suited Will. He wanted very much to be out of Mr. Nichols' company for a while. John seemed to be quite at ease. He was in his fourth year as the cobbler's apprentice, and none of it was too new for him, he said, because his father and grandfather had been shoemakers.

As a child he had played with shoemakers' tools—the tools which now so bewildered Will Carey, and he took time to explain each one with its use in the trade.

"You fourteen?"

"Yes."

"Splendid age to begin. The muscles in your hands can learn better now than earlier or later. Don't be too cut up; it's not a bad thing to make something useful, like shoes that every man needs. I'll help you, Will, and you'll get used to Mr. Nichols' sharp ways of saying things."

"He said one nice thing. Something about a pork pie."

"Two. He'll feed you well."

"I didn't see any kitchen."

"No. I guess this workroom was it when the house was built. There's really not much need, for Mr. Nichols has no wife. He goes to the tavern for his dinner, and brings in something for me, or sends me down the lane to the pastrycook's. It's easy to buy summat already cooked. He keeps tea and ale a-plenty. I bring fruit from home. The porridge pot's always put near the fire, evenings, and we have that for breakfast."

"That's good news. How old are you, John?"

"Just turned seventeen. You know, I've seen you in Three Ravens at Paulerspury. My folks live at Yardley-Gobion, just past Paulerspury. I've walked through your parish many a time, coming here."

"You walk?"

"Why not? After six days at the bench I could walk forever, to stretch myself."

"I like it, too. I always want to be outdoors." He hesitated, then confided, "I meant to be a farmer, but every time I worked in dirt, or got near certain plants, I got something wrong with my skin, bad wrong. I sneezed and sneezed."

The pork pie was good. The two boys licked their fingers clean. "Get your hands dry, and I'll give you lesson one," John said. Will rubbed his palms on the seat of his breeches.

John picked up his awl. "This is mine. You'll have your own. People like different shapes to the point. I use a diamond point. Mr. Nichols prefers a rounded one. Even a good awl will break against harsh leather, so the point has to be kept very sharp."

"How?"

"Oh—sandpaper, a whetstone, the leg of a boot—anything to brush it clean. Can you 'sew a fine seam,' like the little girl in the nursery rhyme?"

"No."

"You'll learn. It's easier if you keep your thread well twisted and waxed. Can you whittle pegs?"

"That I can do. Why pegs?"

"They're used in soles. From three to eight to the inch. Mr. Nichols buys hard maple wood for them. Well, I won't put you to whittling yet, until Mr. Nichols gives us our instructions, but here, try scraping this hide. That's a beginner's task."

Will tried to keep his nose from wrinkling as he smelled the hide. He wanted to please John. The moon-shaped knife for hide-scraping was different from any Will had ever held, but he soon caught on to the strokes and devoted his whole attention to doing it well.

Before he realized it, Mr. Nichols was in the shop. "Glad to see you're not wasting time. There's hide-scraping enough to last you all afternoon."

Candles lit the gabled attic that night while John showed Will where to keep his things. There were two narrow beds, two chests, two chairs, one little table. With the two boys the space was more than full. However, Will liked having someone to talk to after he went to bed. He did not feel so small after he found out that John could not read, and had, in fact, never been to school.

" 'Tis easy. I'll teach you. We'll trade reading for cobblin' lessons. I owe you one already."

"It's a fair trade. And what's your religion, Will? Church of England, I suppose?"

"As far as it's anything. I've had about enough of religion. My fa's the parish clerk and he's seen to it that I never missed a service. What's yours?"

"I can't rightly say. But I think on't a lot. My folks are freethinkers. I guess your fa'd call them nonconformists

—they're outside the Church of England in all they believe and do. My grandsire, a shoemaker, had to leave his town of Caversfield because of his religion. He loaded all his shoemaker's tools, and hid a pulpit under them, and moved to Yardley-Gobion where he could worship as he wished. He's dead now, but my parents think his way. That's why I got no schoolin'. Children of dissenters aren't allowed."

"I've seen that little Paulerspury chapel near Yardley-Gobion," said Will.

"No doubt. And there's a meetinghouse like it near Piddington, in the Hackleton hamlet. I go there when I can get away."

"Does Mr. Nichols object?"

"Oh, me! He does object, indeed. He's a strong churchman, himself. Church of England, that is."

"My fa' satisfied himself of that before he signed me over."

John smiled wryly. "You should hear some of his 'churchman's' language and see him cross and fussy when he comes in tipsy, on Saturday nights."

"No doubt I shall."

The candles sputtered and were spent. Rain began to beat on the roof just above them. Will pulled up his cover. Presently he whispered, "John?"

"Ummmm—yes?"

"I'm thinking of your grandsire. He must have been a

brave man to leave his home, just for religion's sake."

"He was."

"And the folk of Caversfield, a mite cruel to want him away. What harm, to have a different belief?"

"Ask Mr. Nichols that, I dare you. He'll have an answer. That man's a great one to argue, so long's he's winning. And about the Church of England, he always wins, for that's the church of our King George, God save him."

"You said that in a funny voice."

"You notice too much, for fourteen. Get some sleep. You've hard lessons tomorrow—all about the awl—ha!"

"Good night."

"G'night, Will. Nice to have you here. It's been lonesome since William Robinson took off. He was a plucky lad, good company, but he couldn't stand the master."

9
Changes Come Fast

Under Clarke Nichols' excellent instruction, and with John Warr's daily help in all the little things which could easily have upset a new apprentice, Will made progress. Cutting, stitching, lining, nailing, rubbing, lacing filled the days. Soon Will discovered that he was delivery and errand boy as well. Getting out of the shop was a pleasure, but it added to his work. He was still expected to complete his stint of indoor work. Mr. Nichols was strict.

The first Saturday he was free to go home, Will got up early and put on his best clothes. As he came down the ladder from the attic, he saw his master waiting.

"Good morning, Will Carey. Figuring to be gone, I see. Before you head for Paulerspury, you'll take Farmer Crimmons' order of jackboots to the blacksmith's, to have their iron pattens put on."

"But—but—Mr. Nichols, do I need to wait at the forge for them to be done?"

" 'Twon't take long, only four pair. Mebbe one of the Crimmons boys'll come this afternoon to fetch them. Wish I could just make shoes, and he get his own ironing done, but he wanted these finished off. Takes a sight of iron to fend off good English mud."

Will saw a good half of his precious holiday vanish. But there was no help for it. He put the shoes in a strong bag and did as he was told. He wore jackboots himself, nearly everybody did, but his had no extra iron on the soles and heels. Uncle Peter used pattens, though, and he said they helped in a muddy field.

Will was restless while the blacksmith worked. When he saw the eighth boot in the smithy's hand, he heaved a deep sigh of relief.

"Soon, now, lad. I'm doing me best."

"I know, sir. I just wish you could put wings on my own jackboots, so's I could get home faster."

"Wings, huh? Wish I could. I'd get a sight of orders if I had that skill. Don't fret, Will Carey. You'll get far on yer own two feet, I'll wager that. Here now, pattens are on. Be off with you."

Will fled, but it was afternoon before he reached the schoolhouse and whisked Mary high in his arms in the joy of reunion.

Uncle Peter came for supper, bringing a sausage roll for Will to take back, but there was no time for the badger-set.

After church on Sunday, Will went straight to the cottage of his friend Thomas Jones, and drew from his belt pouch a small piece of paper with many words copied on it.

"This isn't Latin, Mr. Jones, but it certainly is not English, either. What is it?"

"It's Greek, Will. Where on earth did you run into that?"

"The master has a fat book called *A New Testament Commentary*. It has a lot of this in it. I want to learn it."

"All, I suppose?"

"Please."

"Now, Will, my Greek days are far behind, and it is a difficult language to remember. But I can dig up a grammar and a glossary, and we'll get started next time you come home. How's the Latin?"

"I get some time to study it, between chores, and at night. Mr. Nichols is generous with candles. I'm ready for a new list in the vocabulary."

"I'm sure you are."

The next Sunday John Warr invited Will to go to the Hackleton prayer meeting with him, and he did. What he saw and heard worried him. The worshipers sat on benches, and they sat wherever they pleased rather than in their own family pew. Everybody sang or prayed, from the heart; there were no prayer books. The preacher wore no churchly robes, and there was no clerk to check the attendance. Yet a warm feeling of friendship—no, more than that—seemed to be in the air.

"How did you like it?" asked John.

"It's not church. And not for me."

Will's conscience hurt him for having gone at all. To make up, he went to three Church of England services during the week. But, because he liked John and because that young man was so sincere, Will accepted other invitations to Hackleton. He wished John would stop asking him, and he could be free of church questions that troubled his mind.

Sometimes Mr. Nichols teased John about his free-thinking parents and his prayer meeting habits. When he had drunk too much wine at the tavern, he scolded John, and insisted that all dissenters were of the devil. This troubled both boys—John, because he was trying to find his own way in his heart, and Will, because he did not want his friend hurt.

Money was a bigger problem to Will than church. He hadn't any. At the forge, a villager had laughingly given him a counterfeit shilling, and he carried this always in his belt, 'for luck.' More and more, Mr. Nichols sent him to buy small supplies, or to deliver shoes and collect his fee. One day he was sent all the way to Northampton, with instructions to bring home a good sum of money for the completed order. In the town, the biggest one Will had ever seen, he spent one of Mr. Nichols' shillings for a bag of horehound sweetballs, and substituted his own false one.

All the way back to Piddington he fretted, wondering whether the master would notice, or if he did, whether he would believe the story that the man who paid for the shoes had included the bad shilling. It was nearly Christmas. Maybe some good will would find its way into the cobbler's heart.

But no. Mr. Nichols noticed. He accused. He did not believe. The fact of Christmas made matters worse, for Will was threatened with being sent home.

"I will not abide a thief, or a liar," declared the man, and Will, deeply frightened and ashamed, sobbed.

Overnight, the shoemaker decided to have mercy on his young apprentice, and keep him. The lesson had cut its way into Will's life. No more did he try to cheat, even in a small way, and it was a long time before he could face Mr. Nichols without turning a dull red.

Events larger than a shilling changed the cobbler's shop at Piddington. A tall young lady, Miss Frances Howes, consented to become Mrs. Clarke Nichols. First, after the marriage, she insisted that a modern kitchen be built off the back of the house, one with a wide fireplace, a brick oven, two hanging spits, and several kettle arms. To the boys' relief, she liked them both and fed them well. They stood in line to help her and run her errands. Two did not make a long line, but it was a willing one.

The bachelor-turned-husband began to watch his tongue, so sharp scoldings became fewer, and work in the shop moved more easily. Will was earnestly polishing a pair of hunting boots, made up for a neighboring squire, when Mr. Nichols came in one morning and praised the boots.

"You saw these boots through, from cutting to shine, did you not, Will Carey?"

"Yes, sir."

"When you think they are ready, put them in the window."

For an apprentice, this was the highest honor. Piddington folk and visitors to the town passed the cobbler's window all day long. Only the finest products from the shop were ever displayed there, and then only one pair at a time. Usually it was Mr. Nichols' own handiwork which was put in full view of the public.

Will's voice broke as he tried to say thank you. He was not sure if that happened because he was choking back some happy tears, or because he was in his middle teens and his words often came out in a different key.

As footsteps paused before the Nichols window and admiring glances fell upon the burnished boots therein, Will rejoiced. John was open in his pleasure for the younger boy, and this doubled the satisfaction. It would be something, indeed, to tell his mother, next visit. He hoped very much that she would in turn tell his father.

Whenever he went to Paulerspury, Will read the *Mercury*. By that time the news was old, so he was surprised to see a public notice at the Piddington tavern proclaiming Wednesday, February 10, 1779, a day of national fasting and prayer, by order of His Majesty, George III. All England was expected to rally in patriotism because the war then in progress in America was going so badly. Men said quietly that the colonists were winning.

"Come with me to Hackleton Meeting House, Will," urged John.

"No. If Mr. Nichols gives us the day off, I shall spend it in his wife's garden."

"You won't be allowed. This is a royal order, to fast and pray."

"Don't like to do either, but to please you, I'll come."

"Come for yourself, not for me. The speaker is a young man, Thomas Chater, from Olney. You may like what he says. I do."

Will had never heard a speaker who seemed so filled with the love of God—and who could make that love so real to others. Thomas Chater spoke earnestly of every man's need of a Saviour. He urged each listener to find God's will for his life.

For a long time Will had felt a lack in his life. He was hungry for something that he did not get in his own church. After Thomas Chater's sermon, he believed he knew what that was.

When the boys got back to their attic, he told John that he wanted to join the Hackleton Meeting, and be a part of their band.

"Do you mean that, Will? Has Christ really come fully into your heart? Do you accept him as your Saviour?"

"Yes, I do, John. In a truly new way!"

For the first time, Will and John prayed together. Then John said, "Now that we feel the same, we must make this known to Mr. Nichols. Maybe we could lead him to share our faith."

Will was aghast. "Lead Mr. Nichols? We could never."

"No, *we* could never. But with Christ as our Helper— anyway, we must try."

"I'm not sure I have that kind of courage."

"We'll ask God for it."

Passing months made this trial more urgent, for Clarke Nichols became ill. Lying in bed, he listened to his two apprentices without interruption as they told what a difference a personal Christ was making in their lives. Through them, he found a closer touch with God, and spoke to other visitors of "Jesus, the sinner's friend."

In September, 1779, after a marriage of only two years, Mr. Nichols died. Will grieved. A year ago he would not have thought that he could, for this man.

John was almost ready to make shoes on his own, but Will had to seek a new place. In the Hackleton Meeting, he had met a cobbler, Mr. Thomas Old, whom he liked.

Right after the funeral, Mr. Old came into the workshop and asked Will if he cared to move in with him, to finish his apprenticeship.

"I'll have to take it up with my father, sir. I think he will be glad not to have to get me located."

"I shall send an invitation to your father to visit me overnight at Hackleton. Naturally he wants to approve the arrangements for his son."

Mr. Edmund Carey came at once, and found a better plan afoot than he had expected. Mr. Old proposed to pay Will a small sum each month, rather than receive ten pounds a year from the schoolmaster.

"I've been watching your boy for some time, Mr. Carey," Will overheard him say. "He is going to be a good cobbler because he is thorough in everything. He leaves no part of the job undone. Will makes sturdy, dependable shoes, and pleased customers will always return. He's not the fastest stitcher in England, but that will come. I'd rather have an honest, steady workman than a quick one. He'll be worth what I pay him; you can count on that."

Praise came hard to Mr. Carey, but he gave a bit, and then he warned Will: "I'd be careful about that prayer meeting group I hear you're mixing with. It's easy to be confused, at seventeen. You'd best think more about what you're doing. Worship at a proper church and in the proper way."

Some of Mr. Old's friends had books which they loaned

to the apprentice who could read. One, called *Help to Zion's Travelers* by Robert Hall, answered many questions which had haunted Will. He saved his shillings until he could buy a copy all his own, and mark it as he studied and restudied.

As he dipped deeper into religious writings, Will found he needed another language, Hebrew. Thomas Jones of Paulerspury threw up his hands and declared he knew no word of it. But another Thomas, a Thomas Scott, who came often to visit Mr. Old, could oblige. He watched the young apprentice with eager eyes, and called the Hackleton cobbler shop "Carey's College."

Mr. Scott was a dissenting preacher who traveled about the English midlands holding meetings. In no other village had he met a lad who made shoes all day and studied Latin, Greek, and Hebrew far into the night.

10
A Globe of Shoe Leather

William Carey's body stopped growing at five feet four inches, but when pretty Dorothy Plackett smiled at him he felt ten feet tall.

As his wedding gift, Will made her a pair of green velvet slippers such as court ladies wore, and lined them with bits of silk from France. They were so beautiful that Dorothy declared she would never wear them.

As the bride was Mr. Old's wife's sister, the young Careys had family help in setting up housekeeping in a thatched cottage of their own. Friends from Hackleton Meeting, too, rejoiced with them. During the first year of marriage, Will cobbled shoes, studied his languages, and planted a garden. A little daughter, Ann, was born, bringing great happiness.

Then all of them fell sick, and the baby died. Dorothy tried to ease her sorrow by nursing Will back to health. She made linseed tea, black currant wine, even pounded white rose petals for a special brew, but Will burned with high fever one hour, shook with chills the next. Mrs. Edmund Carey came from Paulerspury to help. Finally, thin and pale, Will began to eat calf's-foot jelly, and to walk again.

From the fever, his hair began to fall. To his dismay, it all came out. He was wearing a cap all day when Willie Hinde, still his friend, came to visit him, with the gift of a little pig, and made a fine suggestion.

"There's an uncommon good barber in nearby Moulton, Will, a Mr. Wilson. Why don't you have him make you a wig? They're a mite sporting for cobblers, I know, but 'tis hardly right a fellow of but twenty-two should be so bald."

"I've heard of Mr. Wilson. He's a Baptist."

"Those 'jangling Baptists,' as folks call them, always causing trouble to the Church. But this one is said to know his trade."

"Don't speak so poorly of them, Willie. They show courage in their belief. I am more than interested in their beliefs."

"Say it not. But what about the wig?"

"I've no money to pay for such. Wigs are for the gentry."

Several days later Uncle Peter came to Will's workshop, and when he left Will had been given the price of a full-sized hairpiece, one that would even be clubbed at the back, tied with a thong of leather, and waved generously on top.

"Did Willie Hinde put you up to this?" asked the young cobbler.

"Willie asked for nothing. He just stated your plight. We're glad to have you still alive, Will. I'm going to send over a cow for Dorothy, one with a new calf, so you can both have fresh milk to build your strength."

"What would have happened to us Careys if you had stayed in Canada, Uncle Peter?"

"Oh, you would have managed. There's an iron will in you, even in troublesome circumstances. Keep your chin up."

"Over a cobbler's lapstone?"

Mr. Wilson, the barber, liked Will right away. Certainly he would be able to make a wig to Uncle Peter's order and the wearer's satisfaction, he declared, and proceeded to take the proper measurements.

"You measure heads; I measure feet," observed Will.

"And I hear you've a deep measure of religion," Mr. Wilson remarked, opening a subject dear to both of them. Will was surprised at the range of Mr. Wilson's education, and was delighted when the barber mentioned a friend, William Cowper. Cowper's poems appeared often in the *Mercury,* and Will admired them all.

"Would you like to go with me to Olney, to call on him, someday soon?"

The prospect of such pleasure helped Will to get well. In his breeze-cooled summer house at Olney, the poet met

the cobbler with genuine welcome. Will had been afraid
that he would say the wrong things in the presence of such
a famous man, but the double rows of pinks and the
myrtle and the green beans in bloom showed that they
had love of flowers in common. Over the teacups and
bannocks, with honey from Cowper's own bees, the three
men talked, and discovered a common interest in religion.

"Did this man tell you that even if he is called to comb
the hair of her Ladyship, the squire's wife, on a Sunday,
he will not go?" asked the poet, with a twinkle.

"He dares say no to the squire?"

"Only the first time was hard," Mr. Wilson said.

"Since then, they've found that Saturday does as well
for hairdressing. I worship, the whole sabbath."

"Can you gentlemen wait here for a bit? I've a new
poem which I want my favorite critic to read before I
send it to the printer. I'm thinking of calling it 'John
Gilpin's Ride.' "

While Mr. Cowper went into his house, Will ques-
tioned the barber about being a favorite critic.

"He claims to value my opinion. I guess I'm a 'general
reader.' I do like what he writes, though, and every few
days he's sending over something to my shop."

To now, Will had known few friends with whom he
could exchange ideas, or who did not work with their
hands, as he did himself. Meeting a poet in his home was
a rare privilege.

"I never thought to be entertained by anyone great," he told Dorothy that evening.

"I think you are great, Will. Don't be afeared of folkses."

But at once Will resolved to learn more. He bought books in French and Italian, and added them to his Latin and Greek and Hebrew volumes. Because they were language cousins to Latin, the new languages were not too hard. Next, he thought, he would try Dutch.

Members of the Hackleton Meeting were simply banded together in belief of religious freedom to worship as they saw fit, but as Will studied his Bible day after day, he became convinced that he himself was a Baptist in spirit. On a chilly October morning in 1783, he rose well before dawn and walked five miles to the river Nene where it flowed gently near Northampton Castle. Waiting for him was a Baptist minister, John Ryland, and a very few friends. At six o'clock he was baptized, by his own choice.

William Carey was the only candidate that morning. The baptismal service was frowned upon in the community. The squire of Northampton Castle would have been displeased had he realized what was taking place nearby.

Soon afterwards Will began to receive invitations to preach in the many villages of the shire. He was surprised to find so many little bands of Baptists, even one in

Paulerspury. Their invitation he accepted, and as he stood before the group, he saw his mother and his sister Ann among them. His father, being a clerk of the Church of England, of course was not seated where he could be seen, but Will learned later that he had been hiding and had listened and was not displeased with Will's sermon from the Scriptures.

That fall Will's world widened when he came across a book called *Captain Cook's Voyages,* with thrilling illustrations. It was the story of a man who, like Columbus, explored new lands. But the captain was an Englishman from Yorkshire. He described in vivid ways the life of peoples in the South Seas. The author described them as like children in some ways, but terrible too, with war as their main sport, and victories celebrated by eating one another. It came to Will that if they knew of Jesus and his love, their lives might be brightened and saved. In his imagination he chartered large ships and filled them with men of noble purpose, that of taking Christianity to those faraway islands. From that time on, every time he prayed, Will mentioned this dream.

For his workshop wall, Will made a map of the world, carefully placing each country and island. Below it, he filled in figures as he could find them. Ninety-nine times he wrote the word "pagan" on certain regions. Fifty-three times he put in "Mohammedan." Where there were no Christians to record, he grieved.

"Men go gladly to the Spice Islands, and to the Indies for trade and gold," he told his friend Mr. Wilson, the barber. "Why, oh, why can they not be fired with the same enthusiasm to go in search of men's souls?"

"There's still work to do in England, Will Carey," said Mr. Wilson. "Moulton, now. Shall I be seeing you there on Sunday?"

"Yes, and hold your surprise, I'll be the one in the pulpit. I can't think why I was asked to preach. I'm not an ordained minister."

"You've a message. Baptists are hungry for truth."

"In my life now I have two purposes—to know the Bible better, and to explain it to others. But I'm so ignorant, so ignorant."

"Some doubt that."

Mr. Old died, and the Careys made new plans. Now William was, in his trade, a "journeyman." This meant that he was skilled enough to take his own orders, make the shoes, and keep the money for his needs. In the village of Moulton, one he knew well, he rented an empty cottage which had been built for a shoemaker. Close to the door there was a stone trough for soaking leather. Willie Hinde came over to help him clear away the ruins of an old barn and plant a garden. Across the village green from the cobbler's shop stood a public tavern. Some years ago this would have pleased Will; now it distressed him. On Sunday the tavern did its liveliest business.

On Lady Day, March 25, 1785, the cottage was sweet and clean, ready for Dorothy Carey and their infant son, Felix. Moulton life was busy. More money was needed for everything—the fishmonger, the greengrocer, and the butcher, though the Careys visited his shop very rarely. William opened a little school at night.

Dorothy was surprised one day to go into the cobbler's shop and find her husband cutting odd bits of leather into unusual sizes, and to see other pieces pinned to a tracing board. They certainly were not the shapes for shoes.

William was delighted to explain. "My little scholars don't understand a map. I told them the story of Columbus today, and they couldn't realize what an adventure he had. I tried to show them on the wall map I made, but it was a flat surface, and not exciting. I plan to read them some of *Captain Cook's Voyages*. They must learn that there is a world outside this English village."

"Yes, but what are you doing?"

"I am making a globe. See, I have cut the continents and the seas all in their proper shapes. Where countries are not too small, I am separating them as well."

"A globe of shoe leather?"

"Why not? I am dyeing the pieces different colors. It will be an inviting world."

In spare hours, which were not many, William worked on his globe. When the continents and oceans were dyed and dried, he stitched them together with utmost care,

using beeswax to rub his thread and needles, so the stitches would be tiny and true. When it was done, he addressed his young students the first night, "Now, young gentlemen, we have before us the world."

From then on, because of the globe, the boys knew the heroic bravery which Columbus and other explorers had shown. Customers who came into the shop commented on it.

"I never saw a cobbler so concerned about the world," declared a coachman who had come to order high boots.

"But we have a duty toward it. Look, there is Tahiti, a beautiful place, tiny on its vast ocean, but filled with men and women, boys and girls who do not know the love of God."

"Never thought of it. I have troubles right here as I go to and from London. I don't know their religion, but highwaymen try to rob my coach many times a year. So these boots, if ye don't mind, must have a pocket inside the lining where I can put the money from my fares. Hide it as well as you can. They sometimes strip me of my coat and pouch, but never yet have they taken off my boots."

"What about a lining of wool's fleece, which will also keep your feet warm?"

"Good. When will they be ready?"

"Today fortnight."

"I'll stop. I'm told you're a man of your word. And, Mr. Carey—"

"Yes?"

"I wouldn't try to carry the world on my shoulders. You're too young."

"It's not on my shoulders. It is in my heart."

Mr. Thomas Gotch of Kettering, a prominent merchant and banker, sought out William and gave him orders for as many shoes as he could turn out. In turn Mr. Gotch sold them to the British Army and Navy. One morning Mr. Gotch, who usually sent an errand boy to pick up the ready boots, came himself. First, he admired the map hung all across the wall, and then the many-colored globe. He told William that they had a mutual friend, the well-educated preacher, Andrew Fuller, his pastor.

"Fuller tells me that you are a rare linguist, Mr. Carey, and are going to make a good preacher, with more experience. How much do you take in in a week, cobbling, including my own orders?"

"About ten shillings, sir."

"Ten shillings. Well, I've got a secret for you. I don't want you to spoil any more of my leather."

Will's heart fell to his feet, but Mr. Gotch was teasing. He went on, "You must get on as fast as you can with that Latin and Greek and Hebrew. From now on, I'll allow you ten shillings a week from my private purse."

"A burden is gone. I'm glad and lightsome," Will reported to Dorothy.

After he was ordained into the Baptist ministry, Carey preached often, and became the regular pastor in Moulton. He considered this "the highest honor upon earth" and wrote to Andrew Fuller: "Preaching, though a great part, is not all of our employ. We must maintain the character of teacher, bishop, overlooker in the chimney corner as well as in the pulpit." In his own chimney corner, Will had been a thorough teacher, for his wife Dorothy, his sisters Ann and Mary, and Ann's husband William Hobson were baptized, and this gave them all much joy.

Soon Ann wrote Will of serious difficulty.

"This day we had a visit from Mr. Ogden, overseer for our squire. He brought the message that do we have another prayer meeting on the squire's land, we must leave our farm. He's strong Church of England, as you know, and impatient beyond reason of Baptists. Will, we pay our yearly rent each and every Christmas time, as others do. Is our cottage not to be our home?"

Will was distressed, and more so when he learned a few weeks later that the squire carried out his threat and William Hobson had to locate another farm. Willie Hinde, too, was in trouble. He joined the Baptists soon after Ann did, and the squire's swineherd swore he would report him.

The Hobsons had to move, for they held another prayer meeting. Religious freedom had limits in England.

11

"Expect Great Things—Attempt Great Things"

"How would you like to live in a real town, Dorothy?" Will asked his wife.

"Move from Moulton? I've scarce stopped missing Hackleton. Must we?"

"The members of Harvey Lane Church in Leicester have called me to be their pastor. 'Tis a fine town of thirteen thousand souls, and oil lamps to light its High Street. London is but twenty hours away by stage; perhaps we can even go there someday."

"Is there a pastor's cottage?"

"A pleasing one, which looks over fields and gardens straight to the river Soar. It has a brick floor in the main room, and a big lean-to kitchen. Upstairs, there's an attic, with plenty of room for the three boys."

"The church, is it really on a lane?"

"No more. Once when Baptists were persecuted there, they could get no permit to meet in town, so they used a barn on a country lane. But this building faces a well-cobbled street, and can seat two hundred at a time. There's a good stipend, forty pounds a year."

"More'n we ever had."

After the move, the forty pounds a year seemed not so much. Food cost more in Leicester. Will, though a pastor, returned to making shoes. He put his cobbler's tools on the brick floor. When his members came to talk about their troubles and to ask their pastor's advice, they smelled wet leather soaking, and while Mr. Carey talked with them he nailed away. Often they knelt by the cobbler's bench for prayer.

Willie Hinde knocked at Will's door early one morning, tired from walking thirty miles through the foggy night.

"He did it, Will. My master reported me to the squire for joining the Baptists, and I've been sent away. 'Tisn't fair. I'm a good pigman, and I've always given honest service. What can I do?" Willie was always excitable, and now tears rolled down his face.

"First, eat and rest." Will brought him a wooden bowl of bread and milk, and Willie devoted himself to breakfast. When the bowl was empty, he rose, stretched, and fingered the shoe-leather globe.

"Made yourself a leather pretty, eh?"

"It isn't a pretty, Willie. It is the world, strange and wonderful. The world in shoe leather! It beckons me, Willie. It beckons me."

"Are the oceans that deep a blue?"

"All I know of oceans is what Uncle Peter told me, and what I read in books. I hope to know someday how blue they are, and who lives on their shores."

"You're an odd one, Will, but a good one. For myself, I'd be satisfied to have a paying living, here in England."

By noon Will had found work for his friend. Harvey Lane Church needed a caretaker, and there was a cubbyhole of a room at the back where Willie could live. He had no wife, and had brought his few clothes in a roll strapped to his shoulders, so he moved right in.

Customers found the cobbler studying different things on certain days. On Mondays he read great books, on Tuesdays, textbooks on science and history. From Wednesday on, he prepared for Sunday, studying his Hebrew Bible and Greek New Testament.

"But you neglect your business," objected a miller who wanted his boots mended in a hurry.

"Sir, spreading the kingdom of God is my business. I only make shoes for a living."

For some reason Will could not understand, people gathered to hear him preach. He was short and he was poor, and his wig seldom kept its expected place on his head. His hands, as he turned the pages of his Bible, were stained and scored by stitching. Yet the words from his lips were touched with sincerity and passion, and his brown eyes seemed to glow with a holy flame.

He preached of missions and missionaries, of John Eliot and David Brainerd who left comfortable homes and ministered through hardship to the American Indians. He told of the vast oceans, with their palm-fringed islands and peoples who had never heard the word of God. These were new ideas to the Baptists of Leicester.

"Why do we baptize?" he asked. "If baptism concerns us, world missions must no less. The two were bidden in one breath. British traders press into the East Indies and Persia, into China and Greenland. Cursed slave raiders dare deep into Africa. Should Christians be less resolved, less adventurous than these?"

In the quiet of his home he searched his own heart as he tended his choice window plants. Surely, as they were meant for sunlight, so man was meant for Christ. He himself wanted to take the Christian message to the South Seas. Because he had read *Captain Cook's Voyages* so often, he thought seriously of Tahiti.

The struggling small Baptist churches of middle England formed the Northamptonshire Association. The association was to meet in May, 1792 in Nottingham and the young pastor of Leicester, William Carey, was asked to preach. As he planned his sermon, eight years of study and prayer and God's leading flowed into his outline.

He chose as his text the words of Isaiah 54:2: "Enlarge the place of thy tent, and let them stretch forth the curtains of thine habitations: spare not, lengthen thy cords, and strengthen thy stakes." A shoemaker, used to doing things in pairs, he chose a subject with a two-pronged thrust: "Expect great things from God; attempt great things for God."

Carey's theme was the spread of the gospel to all the world, far beyond Northamptonshire, beyond England. His words struck like lightning, with a result of verbal thunder. Older, influential men were moved to agree with him. Andrew Fuller, a powerfully built former boxer who had given his life to the Lord, rose to stand beside the little cobbler with the vision of the world. John Ryland, who had baptized William in the river Nene, wrung his hand as he said, "A deathless sermon! A deathless sermon!"

"Noble," Andrew Fuller declared.

"But is nothing to be done, sir?" asked William Carey.

Something was done. On the second day the association passed a resolution: "That a plan be prepared against the next ministers' meeting in Kettering, for forming a Baptist Society for propagating the gospel among the heathen."

Such a plan called for activity. For his church in Leicester, Carey had prepared a study titled "An Enquiry into the Obligation of Christians to Use Means for the Conversion of the Heathen." In it he presented a program, straightforward and simple: pray, plan, pay. As part of the plan the "Enquiry" was printed and circulated among Baptist churches.

On October 2, 1792, the ministers gathered at Kettering. Before the formal meeting opened, they met in the home of Thomas Gotch, a deacon in Mr. Fuller's church. Thomas Gotch was already a champion of Carey's dream. It was he who had given William the ten shillings a week so he could spend more time on Greek and Hebrew.

Five outstanding ministers of Northamptonshire Association, with seven other pastors and deacons, most of them humble men, seemed a small task force to launch a missionary enterprise, but such was their intent. They preached to one another at the church all day. Then they went for dinner to the "Gospel Inn," run by Mrs. Beebe Wallis, a Baptist widow. After a good meal of pigeon pie and treacle pudding and dark strong tea, they moved into Mrs. Wallis' back parlor to discuss the "Enquiry."

Carey explained it fully, urging again, "plan, pray, pay," all without ceasing.

Andrew Fuller supported him. So did Samuel Pearce of Birmingham, John Ryland of Northampton, and John Sutcliff of Olney. Others were sincerely afraid to venture in missions beyond their own churchyards.

"We are too inland and isolated, we Baptists, too poor to undertake an overseas effort," objected one pastor.

"We are nobodies, with no respectability. Among us there is not one squire to take the chair," another added.

"In God's sight we are somebodies," insisted Carey, "with all the respectability of a Saviour's grace."

Faith proved stronger than fear. A society was, indeed, organized, and it was called "the Particular Baptist Society for the Propagation of the Gospel amongst the Heathen." Andrew Fuller was elected secretary, Reynold Hogg, treasurer.

"We can take an offering now, our first, for foreign missions" suggested Mr. Fuller, picking up a snuffbox from the chairman's table. Some of the men had to write a pledge, as every spare shilling had already been spent for the journey to Kettering. Gifts and pledges, though, when counted, added up to thirteen pounds, two shillings, sixpence.

Mr. Ryland's glance fell on the snuffbox lid, and the others gasped when he called attention to the engraving thereon. It was a picture of the conversion of Paul the apostle.

From that October day, Northamptonshire Baptists preached and wrote and talked missions. The idea spread like a brush fire to the other five associations of Baptists in England. Contributions, large and small, poured in. Carey himself promised four guineas a year, though it meant longer hours of cobbling. Already he was saving a tiny bit of money by giving up sugar, in protest of the cruel slave trade in the West Indies. He urged his family and friends to forego sugar, too, and give the shillings they saved to help the mission cause.

Now that the plan had been turned into activity, the

time was at hand to name the Society's first missionary. None of this was to any purpose unless someone really went.

William Carey wanted to be that man. He wanted to be sent straightway to Tahiti.

12
India Beckons; Will Volunteers

For weeks William Carey dreamed of becoming a missionary to Tahiti in the South Seas.

Then he received a letter which changed his direction. It bore a London postmark, and came from a stranger, Dr. John Thomas, who wrote about India with contagious enthusiasm.

Dr. Thomas stated that he was a missionary in every way but name. He had gone out to India as a ship's doctor, and had stayed in Calcutta and other cities of Bengal for several years to heal and preach. Now he wished to return. On reading about the new Society, he had decided to offer himself as its first missionary. He proposed that he and William Carey go out to India together. He was certain that they could support themselves after a year or two when they had become accustomed to the new country.

Carey read and reread Dr. Thomas' letter. He felt joy that someone, anyone, longed to be a missionary. He felt disappointment that he himself would have second place —perhaps no place—in the beginning of the venture. Moreover, he was puzzled by an offhand sentence in the letter: "I had meant to attend the meeting in Kettering, but I forgot." How could a serious person "forget" such an important occasion?

Quickly another meeting was called. This time Dr. Thomas arrived limping on a sprained ankle, but full of information about India's piteous need, idol worship, shocking customs. He described the hideous practice of "suttee" which made a widow lie on her dead husband's funeral pyre and be burned alive. Then he told of countless opportunities for Christian witness which had been open to him because he was a doctor, and he said that his "pundit" (the Indian name for a teacher) wanted someone to come soon who could translate the Bible into Bengali, the language of the people.

William was thrilled. His experience in language study would be of immediate value. If he went, he could apply himself to Bengali as he had to Latin when it was a new undertaking. He turned to Andrew Fuller and whispered, "For eight years I have prayed about this matter, and for the first time I am looking upon a real missionary's face."

Mr. Hogg, the treasurer, pressed Dr. Thomas for information about ways a man could earn his own way in India, and the doctor replied, "Why, living's cheap. One can buy fowls for a penny, a duck for tuppence, and for eighteen shillings build an excellent house with mud walls and a straw roof."

This was exactly what Will had hoped. Without more ado, he volunteered. There were prayers of thanksgiving and hymns of faith. Then Andrew Fuller asked, "Dr. Thomas, will there be difficulty about you gentlemen, with your families, entering India as missionaries? I have read that the East India Company claims the right to issue permits to land there, and that they only want people engaged in trade."

Dr. Thomas wrinkled his brow a bit, then responded. "Yes, there may be difficulty at that point, but I have a friend, Mr. James Savage, who is in India House, and has some influence. I believe that if God wills us to go, the possibility of transportation and means of living in India will be provided."

The meeting broke up with optimism. Mr. Hogg was instructed to make a trip to London to see about passage. William could hardly wait to get home to Leicester to tell Dorothy that they would soon be off to India.

When Will, excited and jubilant, poured out his news, Mrs. Carey simply stared at him. Finally, she asked, "Are you out of your senses?"

He explained, argued, pleaded, entreated. She refused to go. Neither husband nor wife could understand why the other was so obstinate.

"Will Carey, we have three boys, Felix, William, and

Peter. What would they do in a foreign land? Soon there'll be another child born to us. Are you asking me to take an infant across the oceans, just because you've set your mind to go?"

His efforts to assure her of God's everlasting love and care were of no use. He wrote to his parents, asking his mother to come and "talk to Dorothy." Mrs. Edmund Carey could not write, but Will's father sent a fast reply, siding with Dorothy, and calling the Indian mission "the folly of one mad."

None of this broke Will's determination to go. He sought understanding and approval from his church members. Many of them objected, in spite of all the sermons he had preached on the Great Commission. In a particularly heated service, one brave deacon rose and said, "God is bidding us make this sacrifice, testing our prayers' sincereness. Instead of hindering our pastor, let us not even be content to 'let him go.' Let us *send* him."

Will decided to follow what he was sure was God's call and command, even if it meant leaving his family in England. Perhaps within a few years he could return for them and let them know, firsthand, what to expect in India. Until that time they would have to be apart.

Dorothy stopped talking to him. A wall of sorrow seemed built between them. Neither could rise above it. She packed her furniture in a baker's wagon to send to her sister's home in Piddington, and it was time to say good-by.

Something changed Mrs. Carey's heart, for in an unexpected gesture she said, "Will, you may take Felix with you. I cannot bear to see you go alone."

This was some comfort to Will Carey, though far from enough. Felix, who was eight, was surprised and overjoyed. He motioned little William and Peter aside, and urged them to keep asking their mother to take them too, someday. It was a sad hour when Mrs. Carey and the two smaller children got into the cart with the furniture and were driven away.

Mr. Carey tried to forget his personal distress when the time came for his last Wednesday night service in Leicester. Fourteen Baptist ministers put their hands on his head in solemn blessing, and pledged their full support. Although Dr. Thomas had stated that not much money would be needed beyond the first year, some of them doubted that, and they did not mean for the beloved cobbler-pastor to suffer.

"We'll hold the ropes in England, while you labor in India," promised Andrew Fuller. Then he led in an earnest prayer for God's guidance "through all the mystery and possibility of this undertaking."

Thursday, William, Felix, and Dr. Thomas took the stage to London. Mr. Hogg had arranged for them to sail on the *Earl of Oxford* within a few days. They needed a little time before sailing to get written landing permits from the East India Company. Mr. James Savage's efforts,

though kindly, had not proved successful. Other businessmen had tried to help in vain. Nobody in real authority
seemed in favor of missionaries in Bengal, especially Baptist ones.

The Sunday in London, William Carey was invited to
preach in Carter Lane Church. After service, a young man
introduced himself as William Ward of Derby, and added
that he was thankful to be in London for this rare opportunity to learn about missions.

"May I walk with you, Mr. Carey, to your next appointment?"

"By all means. And what is your business, Mr. Ward?"

"I am a printer, sir."

"How old are you?"

"Twenty-four."

Carey laid his arm across Ward's shoulder and said, "I
hope, by God's grace, to have the Bible translated and
ready for the press in four years. You must come and print
it for us."

"I'll be there."

Sailing permits were not granted, but Dr. Thomas per-
suaded Captain White to let the missionary party board
his ship without them. There were seven traveling together—Mr. Carey and Felix, Dr. and Mrs. Thomas and
daughter, and two Thomas cousins who were going along
for the trip.

The *Earl of Oxford* left harbor on time, April 4, 1793,

but within a few hours she dropped anchor and sat riding the heavy waves. Mr. Carey sought out the captain to ask why.

"We've a wait here, for other ships going around Cape of Good Hope to gather. There's piracy on the high seas. 'Tis far safer to travel in a convoy. You may leave the ship if you like. We may be here several weeks."

They were there six weeks. Mr. Carey got a small room for himself and Felix in the tiny village of Hyde on the Isle of Wight. There, by letter, he learned that a fourth son had been born in Piddington, and that Dorothy had named him Jabez, for a man in the Bible.

Dr. Thomas, alas, had not sailed far enough away from his London creditors. They hunted him "like a partridge," he complained to William. Evidently he had forgotten to pay his bills in the same easy manner that he had forgotten the important Kettering meeting. One large debt of over a hundred pounds took him back to London. There he borrowed from friends, and returned unembarrassed to the *Earl of Oxford*.

The sight of Dr. Thomas, still cheerful, was a great relief to Mr. Carey, but the relief was brief. The morning after the doctor's return, a sailor brought a note from Captain White, requesting both missionaries to appear in his cabin at two that afternoon. They arrived on time, wondering why they had been summoned.

Captain White made a simple statement: "I must ask

you gentlemen to remove yourselves and your baggage from the ship."

There was silence while Captain White seemed to grit his teeth and seek for words. Will Carey's mind began a run-through of his baggage. Had any of his seeds or books or meager clothing been searched and found objectionable?

"For what reason, Captain?" asked Dr. Thomas.

"I am not accustomed, sir, to explaining my commands, but in this special case I shall do so. I dare not risk my ship and the chance that I am not permitted to unload my cargo because I have taken two unwelcome citizens to Calcutta.

"You have no permits to enter Bengal. In fact you have been denied them, you know that, and advised not to make this voyage at this time. The East India Company is too powerful for me to defy them. After careful thought, I must decline to transport you."

"But we are following the call of God," said Mr. Carey.

"Not on the *Earl of Oxford,* sir." Captain White turned to Dr. Thomas. "I will take your wife and family. They are already established aboard, and will pose no difficulties since they are listed as world travelers, not missionaries. I suggest now that after you separate your baggage and get it cleared from the hold, you return to London and try to get your papers in order with the officials."

Except for Dorothy's refusal to come with him, this was

the greatest disappointment of William Carey's life. He was near to tears, and as he bade Captain White a courteous good-by, his voice broke.

"I'll fix it," Dr. Thomas assured him.

Back to London.

"Other ships go to Calcutta. We'll go to a coffeehouse I know, and ask about Scandinavian sailings. The Danes have a settlement near Calcutta," said Dr. Thomas. When they reached the coffeehouse, he asked a waiter's help. The waiter scribbled on a card "a Danish East Indian man, 10 Cannon Street." Those were life-giving words.

At Cannon Street they met a Mr. Smith, who told them that the *Krön Princessa Maria*, owned and captained by his brother, had sailed from Copenhagen. In about five days she would put in at the port of Dover. Yes, she had room for some passengers.

"What shall we do now, Fa'?" asked Felix, who had been quiet throughout all the arrangements.

"You and I are going to Piddington on the first stage."

"I'm coming with you," said Dr. Thomas. "Perhaps I can persuade Mrs. Carey to come with us now."

"If anyone can, you can," William agreed.

Again Dr. Thomas used the magic of words to influence a person. Sobbing, he told Dorothy of the six lonely years he had spent earlier without his family in India, and said, "If you refuse to go now, you'll repent as long as you live."

At last she cried, "I'll go if my sister will go with me."

Catherine Plackett slipped upstairs to her bedroom to pray. When she came down, she announced that she was willing to go.

There was a frantic day of selling, packing, deciding what to take, and what to leave. Willie Hinde came to help with the baggage. The little boys made great plans for the boat trip. Felix told the others about his days on the *Earl of Oxford* and about swinging in a hammock on the ship at night.

Andrew Fuller, delighted that Dorothy had changed her mind, worked tirelessly trying to raise money for more fares. He secured two hundred and fifty pounds, but it was not quite enough.

Dr. Thomas had a suggestion. "Miss Plackett, would you be willing to book passage as a servant? I certainly am, and if we save money by purchasing cheaper tickets, Mr. Fuller has enough for us. I think he has asked everyone he knows already."

"Yes, I'll book as a servant if it will help," Catherine said. "After all we have been through, we cannot let the want of a few pounds stand in the way now."

They made it in time to Dover. At three in the morning, June 13, all eight were in a rowboat, heading for the lights of the anchored *Krön Princessa Maria*. By five they were sailing with a fine fair wind.

When bells chimed for evening tea, William went down the ladder to eat. But suddenly he was not hungry.

"I beg to be excused, sir," he asked the Captain, and rushed to the deck. His head was spinning like a globe. Sharp clear air with no food smells eased the queasy, tossed-about feeling, and he leaned quietly against the deck rail, cherishing the truth that he was really at sea.

As the *Krön Princessa Maria* moved farther from England, Will thought of the home that he had known. He remembered the shoe-leather globe, with its deep blue oceans, its brilliant islands. He remembered how carefully he had cut out leather to represent the shorelines of India and the blue water areas that washed those shores. Now he would see those waters with his own eyes, and his shoes would trudge those shores.

At bedtime Will unpacked his diary, for the first entry of the voyage. As he wrote, his hand quivered, for his body was still not used to the pitch of the waves. But his heart was firm and his course was set. The words he chose glowed with his thanksgiving: "This has been a day of gladness to my soul. I was returned to England that I might take my family with me and enjoy all the blessings which I had surrendered to God."

13
In Tiger Country

In the London office of the Danish shipping company, the captain of *Krön Princessa Maria* was listed as "J. Smith." However, on shipboard, he asked his passengers to call him by his real name of Captain Christmas. Felix, William, and Peter Carey thought him a splendid, jolly friend.

Captain Christmas was courteous and kind, eager to make all the Carey family comfortable. Though Aunt Catherine and Dr. Thomas had signed on as servants to save some pounds, he would not treat them as servants. He invited them to eat at the captain's table with the others. When Sundays came around, he asked Mr. Carey to hold services. Instead of thinking the little band foolish to be going to India as first missionaries, he honored them for it. Twice each day, during the whole voyage, he assured himself that they wanted for nothing.

Early on, everyone was seasick, but soon they got used to the swing of the hammocks and roll of the sea. Baby

126

Jabez thrived, proving himself a stout little sailor and cap-
turing the love of his fellow travelers.

Dr. Thomas began to teach William Carey some words
of Bengali, the language he would have to use at once. In
turn, Mr. Carey taught it to his two older sons. Felix was
excited to be a language student; his enthusiasm reminded
his father of his own first taste of Latin.

Winds took the *Krön Princessa Maria* off course, nearly
to the shores of Brazil. One noonday the Carey boys were
leaning over the rail, watching the sea. Suddenly they saw
a whole herd of porpoises leaping gaily beside the ship,
turning fancy somersaults in the air, and seeming to call
to one another with a high-pitched squeak. At dinner,
later, they told about this sporting show.

"There'll be whales, too, and flying fish, and 'Mother
Carey's chickens,'" said Captain Christmas.

Little Peter Carey choked on his tea, he was so amused,
and repeated, "Mother Carey's chickens?"

The Captain was glad to explain. Even the studious
adults listened with interest. "That's a name the sailors
give to some dark sea birds with long wing spans, the ones
properly known as petrels. Because they need strong winds
to lift them off the waves, they appear as bad weather sets
in, and we call them 'stormy petrels.'"

"But why 'Mother Carey's chickens'?" asked Felix who,
like his father, cared about words.

"Know any Latin?"

"No, sir. Not yet."

"Well, learn this much today. 'Mother Carey' comes from *mater cara* which means 'beloved mother.' These birds are said by sailors to have protection from Mary, the mother of Jesus. No truth to it, just a legend, but the birds are real."

The cabins were hot and stuffy. On the narrow deck, off the southern tip of Africa, a stiff breeze teased William and Dr. Thomas as they bent over notebooks and Bibles. With a lurch of the ship, William's wig left its uneasy perch and slid down over his forehead.

"I'm tired of this thing," he declared and, walking to the rail, pitched it overboard. Dr. Thomas was shocked.

"The people of India will have to take me as I am," said William. "Wigs are fashionable, and for a while I certainly thought I needed it, but I can't be bothered with it the rest of my life."

The top of his head was bald, but hair had grown back around the sides, and what was there was a pleasant brown, somewhat lighter in color than his eyes. His face had lost the winsomeness of youth, but it showed fine character. The bones of his jaw were strong, his lips firm and full, and the dimple in his chin would never change.

"I'm glad that wig's gone," said Dorothy. "You are much handsomer without it. At least we know now where it is. On your head, we could never be sure. Shall I throw the carrying box overboard, too?"

It took five months less two days to reach Calcutta. For the last month, they were within two hundred miles of it, but contrary winds and currents kept the *Krön Princessa Maria* in the Bay of Bengal. Then the winds changed. From weeks of seeing no ships at all, suddenly the passengers found themselves in the midst of craft with strange flags, all making for port.

On November 9, Captain Christmas announced that they were in the mouth of the Hooghly River, and that passengers who did not wish to enter Calcutta by ship could board a smaller vessel. This meant Dr. Thomas and the Careys. They had no wish to meet officers of the British East India Company yet, since they had come without entry permits.

Expertly, Dr. Thomas signaled the master of a dhow which was bobbing busily beside the Danish merchantman, and bargained a price to put them ashore. One by one they went down a rope ladder onto the tiny deck of the bouncy dhow, waved good-by to Captain Christmas, and soon saw a dim gray line of land.

"We'll tie up at a *ghat*—their word for a landing place —and wait for a favorable tide to boost us nearer Calcutta," said Dr. Thomas, after conversation with the Indian captain.

"How long? I'm hungry," put in little Peter Carey.

"Fine. I'll see that you have your first *chupatti*."

"What's that?"

"A little fried cake, crisp and tasty."

Near the ghat, people were milling about, buying and selling, but when they saw two English *sahibs,* two *mem-sahibs,* and four little fair-skinned boys, they came close to examine the odd strangers.

Dr. Thomas began to preach, in Bengali. This was the first time William Carey had seen with his own eyes and heard with his own ears a Christian witness to "the heathen." As the listeners begged "more, more," he hardly knew that three hours were passing. To him it was a blessed occasion, making all the trials of leaving home seem small. He resolved to study all the harder, so he could add his voice to that of his friend.

Dorothy and Catherine and the children stared about them. Dr. Thomas had told them that men wore loose, baggy trousers called *dhotis,* and there they were. Girls and women had on *saris,* long pieces of colored cloth wrapped gracefully around their bodies. Many had nose rings, and heavy silver bracelets or anklets. Others peeped out from veils across their faces. All of them chewed a red kind of nut, which stained their lips and teeth. Little children stood naked, or with short blouses, nothing else.

A man clothed in rags had a live snake hanging around his neck. Dirty white humpbacked cows moved lazily among the people. Dogs nosed for food or waste. A camel loaded with saddlebags of rice picked its dignified way down a path. Over everything, crows cawed and beat their black wings, ready to scoop up any morsel that touched the ground and was not seized by the unpleasant dogs.

Mrs. Carey wrinkled her nose and turned to her sister in distress. "I don't think I can stand this smell, Catherine. Look at that wall, plastered with little cakes of cow dung, drying. And at those women squatting there, patting them out. How can they ever?"

"Try not to mind, please, Dorothy. Look instead at the ones cooking on the little charcoal braziers, and whiff that spicy curry fragrance rising with the smoke."

"Have they no kitchens? Must they always cook outside?"

"We'll find out. I think the courtyard is the Indian kitchen. And in hot weather, probably the eating place. Oh, see the beautiful brass bowl that woman has for her rice. And look, she is serving her children on leaves."

At Bandel, a Portuguese settlement thirty miles north of Calcutta, Dr. Thomas rented two small rooms for his friends, then took off to Calcutta to locate his own family. Soon he was back, smiling as always, and taking William out each day in a rowboat so he could see the countryside. Everywhere they stopped, he preached.

"Ten thousand ministers would not be enough," William estimated, surprised at the throngs of people who surrounded them.

"Your Bengali will soon outreach mine, and you can

give a full sermon instead of a few phrases, for I have arranged that my old *pundit* come to help you, at once."

"Ram Ram Basu?"

"The same. He is really not a Christian, but he understands what we are trying and hoping to do and say. He is a scholar, able to guide you in language, customs, Indian writings. I suggest that you employ him if you like him. He knows some English, and can give Dorothy advice, too, about home things."

Ram Ram Basu came, was invited to join the family as pundit for forty rupees a month, and soon became an important link between the Careys and their new world. Dr. Thomas returned to Calcutta to set up medical practice and make some needed money.

Within weeks he returned, this time with a long face and apologies. To rent a fine house, such as a doctor required, and to pay for his family's keep between their arrival on the *Earl of Oxford* and his own, he had—ah—used all the funds of their "venture," and there would be no more until some arrived from England, promised for next year. William was shocked into harsh words.

"Don't be too troubled. I've a friend who lends money, one Nelu Datta. I have already seen him, and he expects you." The doctor tried to soothe him.

"I have been poor, but I have never borrowed in my life," responded William. "I can make shoes."

"Not here, I fear. The Indians do it, right in the street,

and cheaper. Most of them go barefoot, or wear simple sandals."

Mr. Carey bought a smooth piece of wood and painted a sign: "Shoes Made and Repaired." He thought of the morning at the blacksmith's shop in Piddington, when he had wished for jackboots with wings so he could get away from his irksome apprenticeship. Actually, cobbling had not been so bad, and knowing a useful skill had often helped him through difficulties. Long ago another missionary named Paul had paid the expenses of *his* missionary journeys by making tents.

Dr. Thomas was right. In Calcutta, there was small call for Will's boots. A few Europeans sought him out, but there was not enough money to feed his family and pay a pundit. Ashamed, William was forced to ask Nelu Datta for a large loan. The Indian was shrewd but kind. He was sorry for the little Englishman who seemed so embarrassed.

"Mr. Carey, sir, I have a humble shack, made of mud and bamboo reeds at the gate of my garden in Manicktolla, a very crowded part of Calcutta. If you wish to put your family there until you can make better plans, I will charge you no rent." Will was touched by the offer and, desperate, he accepted.

Though November was Calcutta's coolest month, the miles between Englishmen were long and wearisome, as William tried to find work. His interest in botany soon became known, and though he got no job, he met interesting fellow countrymen.

The government was seeking settlers for a timberland called the Sundarbans. On promise to clear land, plant crops, and build a dwelling, the head of a family would be assigned a plot. William applied for this, and it was granted. On borrowed money he hired a boat to move his family.

"William, when can we have bread? I'm so tired of this rice, and such a little bit for the children," murmured his wife.

"God will not forsake us," William assured her. "He brought us here."

He needed all his faith when their boat pulled onto the ghat at Debhatta in the Sundarbans. It was a wild place, the sloppy landing strip surrounded by thick jungle.

"But—but—William, I don't see a house," said Dorothy. "Did you not ask if there was one?"

"My agreement was to build one. You heard me say that when we discussed coming. I'm sure there's some sort of village near the ghat. I'll look for smoke, and locate it."

Ram Ram Basu made a short excursion on shore, and came back with a long face. "Tiger country. The children must play near you, and nobody sleep out at night."

"Did you find anyone?" Felix asked.

"Yes, a villager fishing. He says that from one Sundarban village not far away, twenty men have disappeared within the year. Bengal tigers. I knew it."

Jabez began to cry, and his Aunt Catherine soothed him. Mosquitoes zoomed around them all. Mrs. Carey and Felix were ill with dysentery, so Mr. Carey unrolled a pallet for them and spread it on the shore. Clouds began to build up, weighty with monsoon rain. The boatman announced that he had to go back to Calcutta.

"No, no," cried out Mrs. Carey. "You must not leave us like this." Then she rose up on her pallet and besought her husband, "William, where are we going to spend the night?"

14
Indigo Adventure

"Look, Fa', I see a man. One like us." Little Peter Carey pointed toward a thicket.

Sure enough, a tall Englishman, followed by a tame dog, came walking toward the water's edge.

"Charles Short here," he introduced himself. "I am salt assistant for the East India Company. We've store-houses—Indians call them 'godowns'—close by. Was just out hunting a bit before the rains break"—he motioned to the long gun in a sling over his shoulder—"but hadn't thought of game like this." The little boys laughed, and William gratefully took the outstretched hand.

On hearing the family's plight, and delighted to have unexpected English company, Mr. Short invited all the family to his large comfortable bungalow, and urged them to stay while Mr. Carey cleared his land and built his little house across the sweet-watered Jubana River. He was a kind host, and knowledgeable about the snake-infested jungle which hemmed them in.

Being near trees with exciting names like banyan, tamarind, sundari, new fruits like mangoes and lichees, outweighed for Carey the alarm about tigers and cobras six feet long. He was pleased, too, to work beside and with the Indians as he felled his logs for a dwelling, and wove a roof of coconut palm fronds. They liked this English *sahib* who seemed more friendly than others. His presence made them fear the lurking tigers less, though they had noticed that he was a poor shot at a deer.

It was a happy, useful time. When he was near certain plants, or worked too long putting out onions in his just-made garden, William sneezed and turned red, as he had done on Uncle Peter's farm. Gradually he learned which plants to avoid, and as Felix got stronger, he took the boy across the river each day with him, to help. Felix had a knack with a hoe, and his skin merely turned a deep bronze in the tropical sun.

During the daily stormy hours, Carey studied Sanskrit, a new language which he was adding to his Bengali. From Sanskrit he expected to go on to many Indian dialects which used it as a base. He relished this form of mental exercise. At night he and Ram Ram Basu burned much of Mr. Short's mustard oil in their lamps, as they pored over books and made translations.

In six months the house across the Jubana was ready. Then came a letter from Dr. Thomas, changing everything. Through a friend, Mr. Udny, he had secured appointments for himself and Carey as managers of indigo "outworks," in faraway Mahipaldighi and Mudnabati. It was God's opening for them to live near each other, to work at translation of the Bible together, he said. The salary would be regular and good, enough to permit them to publish the Scriptures at their own expense when the language part was well done. Instantly, Carey accepted.

Charles Short's face turned pale when he was told that his friends were about to leave. Promptly he asked William for a private conference.

"Mr. Carey, sir, I ask you for the hand of Miss Catherine Plackett in marriage. Until you came to Debhatta my heart was empty. Indians called me the 'salt sahib' and thought my life very fine, but I was lonely. With Miss Catherine I shall not mind staying in the Sundarbans, surrounded by jungle and visited hourly by monkeys. She says she likes it here, and . . . "

"I doubt if the geography and the jungle make any difference to her, Mr. Short. It is you, yourself, she esteems. I do give my full consent to your marriage, but I am sure it will be a blow to my wife. She did not come willingly to India until Catherine promised to come with her."

Catherine stayed behind, to become Mrs. Charles Short, and the Careys took a boat to Mudnabati.

This time a nice bungalow was ready for them. It was

built like an English house, but it had wide piazzas, and each room had a three-bladed fan in the high ceiling. A long cord for pulling and working the blades made fun and games for the Carey boys. They were always glad to stir up a breeze for their mother. Usually it was so very hot they left all doors open.

Mrs. Carey was constantly frightened by a large crocodile which lived in a pool close by. The boys did not mind him.

With botany his deepest interest except religion, William Carey set about learning as much about indigo as he could. Already it was the season for the workmen to bring in bundles of the plants to the vats. They were piled gently into the first vat to soak until the water was an almost black dark green. At exactly the right moment, this water was let into a second vat, where workmen beat it with paddles to force air into the liquid until it turned a bright blue. The skin of the beaters also turned blue, and they were a sight to see. Grains of sediment settled at last to the bottom of this vat; the water was run off, and the remains dried. The dried material was cut into bars, and sent to Calcutta to be sold as a very fine dye. From there it was sent on to England.

Indian indigo made many a fortune.

About some things, Dr. Thomas proved right. Having a friend for a neighbor was delightful. After the first few months, William found that he could arrange time to study, and go out into the country with Dr. Thomas and Ram Ram Basu on preaching tours. Nobody dared accept Christ publicly, but usually listeners were polite.

Carey wrote home to England about this new occupation as an indigo manager, and since he was given use of much land, asked for "a few instruments of husbandry, scythes, sickles, ploughwheels, and an assortment of all garden and flowering trees, also of fruit, field and forest trees, for the lasting advantage of what I now call my own country."

Two years after he reached India, Carey received his first letters from home. Missionary enthusiasm, they reported, was still high in the English midlands. Harvey Lane Church was prospering. His mother was dead, his father married again. Mary could walk no more, and was living with the Hobsons, who took gentle care of her.

These things Will had known would come, and he had prepared his heart to accept permanent separation from loved ones. But he was deeply hurt by letters from several Baptist minister-friends who scolded him for his indigo work, saying that it would take time from his spreading of the gospel.

Had their wives ever been hungry, Will wondered. Had their children slept in fear of prowling tigers because there was no house with walls to shelter them?

After he prayed, William realized that the friends who had misunderstood his actions were half a world away, that the upsetting letters were a full year old, and that not one of the men in England knew that the money they had raised to provide for the first hard years of the Indian mission had been lightly handled by Dr. Thomas.

Sorrow deeper than words touched the Carey home. Bright little Peter, who already spoke Bengali like Indian children, became ill suddenly and died. His mother was inconsolable.

"Were we home in England, I could have made him willow bark tea. It would have brought that fever down," she mourned.

The villagers refused at first to dig the small grave. It was against their religion, they said. Finally four did, and their families were angry. The four came to Mr. Carey for food, for their evening rice had been denied them in their village.

Soon after Peter's death, floods came. Men had to go about in little boats with one sail. The rice paddies were no use, and there was no harvest of grain. Rains kept falling, long after the monsoon season was past.

One morning Mr. Carey heard his wife scream, and he ran to the door of the bungalow where she stood like a statue. Outside, looking ready to lumber up the few steps, was a crocodile, muddy and evil-eyed. Dorothy cried all day, wanting to go home.

The year after the flood, no rains came at all. The crops dried up. Insects ate the tree leaves. The tanks which usually held reserve water for the indigo vats became parched open slabs of mud. Indian women and children went to wells where they normally got water for cooking, and came away puzzled because there was none.

Indigo was supposed to make money for its producers, but in times like these Mr. Carey could report no gain. Instead, there was loss. He knew well that the works could not remain open much longer, and he was discouraged.

One day when he was too worried to study, even, he looked up from his table and saw an English face. He was not expecting company, but here was a fine-looking young man.

"I am John Fountain, Mr. Carey. I have come to help you. And do you remember a young printer, William Ward, whom you met in London? He is on his way."

Every letter that William had written to England had pleaded for more missionaries, but mail took so long, and so often got lost, that Will had begun to feel out of touch with the Society. Never, though, had he felt out of touch with God.

John Fountain stood before him, a living answer to his prayers.

15
Bibles and Butterflies from Serampore

"We shall accept the invitation of his Excellency, Governor Bie, and remove ourselves to the Danish colony of Serampore," William Carey told his family.

Mrs. Carey's eyes sparkled for a moment, then grew dull. She made no comment.

"I remember Serampore. It's near Calcutta, and has big clean houses and tall trees," said little Will, who had been but five on his only visit there. His father was proud that such a small lad had noticed trees.

"Do I remember it?" asked Jabez.

"Hardly. You were a baby," Felix answered him.

"I'm not a baby now, though. I'm a big brother. We have Jonathan. I wish he didn't cry so much."

Mr. Carey wished the same. Jonathan was such a wee fellow, and seemed to digest only rice gruel. He and his mother always looked very sad. Perhaps Serampore would bring new comfort and happiness to them both.

Until Governor Bie wrote to offer a welcome, things

had been uneasy at Mudnabati. Three years of no money profit meant that the indigo works would be closed, and Mr. Carey had been so informed. Dr. Thomas had long since left his post, had been roving from village to village preaching or doctoring or planting. For months his friends had heard nothing about him at all.

Already at Serampore, waiting for Mr. Carey to tell them what to do, were new missionaries sent from England to enlarge the force—Mr. Ward and his bride, Mr. and Mrs. Marshman, teachers, Mr. and Mrs. Brunsdon, Mr. and Mrs. Grant, and a beautiful young woman who was engaged to marry John Fountain.

As their hired boat made its downstream way from North Bengal to Serampore, there was time for rest and singing. Like William Carey, John Fountain had been, as a child, in a boys' choir. In Mudnabati he had taught Felix and young William to sing parts. The Indian boatmen rowed to the rhythm of their hymns, while Mrs. Carey rocked Jonathan in her arms, and stared silently ahead.

"Do you know, I hope to write Christian songs in Bengali, or anyway translate some good ones," said John. "Now—let's sing my favorite from Isaac Watts." In his clear tenor he pitched a true note. Even Ram Ram Basu joined in.

> Come, we that love the Lord,
> And let our joys be known;

Join in a song with sweet accord,
Join in a song with sweet accord,
And thus surround the throne,
And thus surround the throne.

Let those refuse to sing
Who never knew our God;
But children of the heav'nly King,
But children of the heav'nly King,
May speak their joys abroad,
May speak their joys abroad.

"Why the sad look when we sing of joy, Mr. Carey?"
John asked.

"I am grieving for those who 'refuse to sing, who never
knew our God'—all those in Mudnabati who stood and
listened to me preach, but never confessed Christ as Lord.
Years ago, I was a cobbler in Moulton, and for my desk
I stitched together a globe. Beside it I placed a chart list-
ing untouched regions of the world. I should have put in
'Mudnabati—Pagan.' "

Suddenly Mrs. Carey entered the conversation. "Yes,
you should. But you had not heard of Mudnabati then.
I wish I never had. Six years in India we've spent, six
hard, long, hot years, and not one convert."

"I know. It grieves me sorely, Dorothy. I can hardly
bear to face our new co-workers after such failure. Spreading the gospel here is like plowing hard rock."

"Not failure, not failure, Mr. Carey!" John Fountain
interrupted. He could not stand to see his friend's face

so sad. "We cannot look into the years ahead. Who knows what seed has been sown in Mudnabati? To me there is great joy that we have on this little boat the whole Bible, almost, translated into Bengali. Only a few chapters from the Old Testament need to be finished, and it will be ready for printing. You have done a magnificent piece of work, there, beyond belief."

"Thank you, John, for your confidence. But it took me six years, when I had only planned for four."

"No matter. It would have taken anyone else sixteen, or forever. I think we should sing again as 'children of the heavenly King.' I am proud, Mr. Carey, to work beside you."

The missionaries waiting at Serampore, guests of Governor Bie, did their share of rejoicing over the Bengali translation. During a few weeks they had found how hard a language it was. They had sad personal news, though. Mr. Grant, young and dedicated, had fallen ill of a fever and died. He had wanted very much to meet Carey and be joined with him in the noble task.

It was a new year, 1800, a new century, and a new happiness for the English missionaries to begin great plans in Serampore. Immediately they agreed that the most important step was to publish the Scriptures. Ward was learning his way in Bengali as fast as he could, so he could set the type correctly. Carey would advance in Sanskrit, translating the Bible into it for a wider reach than Bengali alone could offer. Mr. and Mrs. Marshman would open a school for children of rich Europeans, charge tuition, and what they made beyond a simple living they would give to the mission for purchase of printing presses and paper.

All of the missionaries wanted to preach the gospel on streets, at *ghats,* in marketplaces, to anyone who would listen. In Serampore itself there were Danes, Germans, French, English, Portuguese, Armenians, Greeks, and persons of all the Indian religions. Most of them understood enough English to attend a service, or to stand near one in curiosity.

The missionaries decided to share everything possible, and to eat together in a large dining room. From the first day everyone understood that guests were welcome, especially for afternoon tea. Sometimes a hundred came to eat, to talk, to question. It was a good way to show Christian friendliness.

Governor Bie gave assistance from his position. The British East India Company, in Calcutta, did not trust these missionaries, but while they were in Serampore under Danish protection, they were safe. A new chapel was built by the Danes, and Carey was chosen pastor. The governor urged his countrymen to send their boys and girls to the Marshmans' school.

Everyone looked to Mr. Carey as their leader. For six years he had made all decisions, except for the money

matters handled by Dr. Thomas. Now his manner was that of a commanding officer, but in his heart he worked at being a member of a team. In Serampore he wanted no jealousy. If each one had a special job, and if all of his little band earnestly sought God's will, he believed that they could create a lively, progressive, consecrated mission.

The mission kept Thursday, April 24, as a thanksgiving day because the family buildings had been completed. There was a sunrise prayer meeting in the walled garden, and a new hymn by John Fountain was introduced. Carey preached in the afternoon, on "Rejoicing in Hope." That very day letters came from England, telling of the Society's satisfaction that so many of the missionaries were together, united in God's purpose. Since everything was going so well, they agreed to open a free school for Indians, each of them giving time as a teacher.

Calcutta Europeans mocked the Serampore group as mad. Carey wrote to his friend, "rope-holder" Andrew Fuller, "Many sneer at us, but we are preparing materials for God's temple in this country, and in him is our confidence."

"How many people live in Calcutta, Will?" asked Dorothy.

"About two hundred thousand. From almost every land. When I go about, I see Chinese, Malays, Burmans, Siamese, all in their national dress, so colorful and interesting. I'd be glad to hire you a palanquin, Dorothy, and take you some afternoon after the heat of the day."

"No, Will. I'll stay here until I die. The only place I want to go is England."

William was grieved that his wife did not enjoy being with people other than her sons and Mrs. Grant, who had become devoted to baby Jonathan. The two ladies sat often in the garden, unless a snake upset Mrs. Carey by showing itself, then she quickly ran indoors.

In Calcutta, William Carey was becoming known. He made friends with outstanding men who operated the botanical garden. Word of his skill at languages spread. Often he was called upon as a translator, in nonreligious matters. Governor Bie told his official associates about the brilliance of the little English missionary, and surprised them by declaring how glad he was to have him and his friends living at Serampore.

Soon after the thanksgiving service, the April moon was full and, for Indian Hindus, it was a festival time. Images of two gods, Radha and Krishna, were sold and carried high on poles by thousands of people in the streets.

Felix had been sent for an order of paper at the warehouse. He came in covered with red powder, and very wet.

"What happened to you?" his brother William wanted to know. "You're a sight."

"I couldn't get through the crowds. Grown-ups, even,

were scattering this red stuff everywhere, and throwing water on each other. There was a parade of camels, with dressed-up riders, and elephants with boys on their heads. I never saw so many bonfires, and people burning paper gods for good luck in the next life. Acrobats were doing rope tricks, and there was a terrible thing, a man hanging from hooks stuck through his skin, not screaming at all. Fakirs threw themselves on spikes. It was all so awful."

As he talked, Felix was stripping. William offered to sluice bath water over him, so they both went into the stone-floored room where tall ewers were kept, always full.

"Bend your head, if you want me to get that powder out," said William, pouring vigorously.

Felix shivered.

"Cold?"

"No. It's that man swinging from hooks I can't get out of my mind. Drums were beat, and the men working the ropes pulled in perfect time. Horrible."

"Felix, have you ever seen a widow burn herself to death on her husband's funeral pyre?"

"No. But Fa' has. He cried. He says if he ever gets any influence in India he's going to see that that custom is forbidden by law." He motioned to his head again, and scrubbed away. "I guess I'll smell it for days. Will, do you remember how in England Mum used to 'heat the copper' and wash us up and down? I'll never feel that clean again."

"D'ye 'spose we'll ever go back to England to live?"

"Never. Fa' came for life. Nothing would turn him back. Nothing."

Dr. Thomas appeared one day that spring, at Serampore, and shortly after, moved with his wife and daughter into a mission house. He had been running a sugar refinery, he said, but unfortunately it had made no money. Now he was ready to give his medical skill and preaching fervor completely to the cause of spreading the gospel.

Knowing Bengali well, often Thomas dressed himself as an Indian and went out in the roads to tell the people of Christ. Once he stopped a Brahman priest and asked whether he knew of anyone in that district who minded God.

"Yes, some foreign *sahibs* do. They speak of one Jesus Christ."

"And who is he?"

"They call him the Son of God."

Telling this, Thomas could assure his comrades that they were building better than they knew. Not only priests, but workers, had heard of that Son of God. One day he met a carpenter, Krishna Pal, who was also a *guru,* or teacher of his own religious truths. The carpenter had questions, and Dr. Thomas urged him to come to Serampore.

On his way, Krishna Pal slipped and fell on a mudbank of the Hooghly River and, in pain, sent to the mission for the foreign doctor. Carey and Marshman went with him.

Next morning, Krishna Pal sought them out again. Soon his physical pain was eased and his spiritual hunger was growing.

On Sunday, December 28, 1800, Krishna Pal was baptized, the first Indian convert of the mission, seven years after it was begun. On that historic morning, William Carey also baptized his oldest son, Felix, so there was double rejoicing in the father's heart.

Felix already lived in Christian surroundings, but for Krishna Pal things were not easy. Because he ate with the missionaries, he was turned away from his family table, and his friends no longer spoke to him, except to mock. The baptism had taken place in the Hooghly, a part of the mouth of the Ganges, India's sacred river. For this Carey was said to have "desecrated the Ganges," and people were angry. They bathed and washed clothes and vegetables in that same river, but it was not the same as having a foreigner to perform a religious ceremony in the name of the Christian God.

In March after the first baptismal service, Ward entered Carey's office and laid a bound printed copy of the Bengali New Testament on his desk.

"Our first, sir. Yours. More will come from the bindery this afternoon."

With trembling hands, William Carey examined it, and found it good. He had translated the New Testament into the simple language of the people, not bookish

phrases. The printing was clear and clean, attractive, inviting. For him, it was the work of seven painstaking years. But without a fine craftsman such as William Ward, who had come all the way from England, it would never have come to finished form.

"We'll send copies to Fuller, Ward. He can use them to stir interest among English Christians. And for us here, this completion of our first task calls for a special thanksgiving. Will you announce it for the chapel tonight?"

One hundred copies were sent to Andrew Fuller, the "rope-holder" in England. With them, Carey also sent a box of Indian butterflies, carefully mounted and labeled. He and Ward had caught them all.

Bibles and butterflies, gifts from an overflowing heart.

16
Calcutta: The World at His Door

"Mail, Mr. Carey, a whole stack of it," said Mr. Marshman, the day after an English vessel came in.

"And only four months old! Why, the ink is hardly dry by the time we see our letters these days."

The men busied themselves reading.

"Listen to this from Andrew Fuller: 'Your gift of Bibles was well received. One of them even reached King George himself, and I understand made a fine impression. Scholars are asking for more information about the subcontinent of India. When they do, I give them your address.' "

"So it appears, from this pile of letters and magazines," Mr. Marshman declared.

"I ordered the agricultural magazines. I want to experiment with Indian soil, to help people here grow their food in the best ways. I get many ideas from these English journals, things my Uncle Peter, who was a farmer, never thought about."

Mr. Carey opened one of the magazines, then said, "You know, I could easily use all my time with plants and trees and flowers and gardens, but when I am tempted to do this, I remember that my main purpose in India is to make God's Word available to the millions in my adopted land."

"You've a deal of reading before you if you give attention to all these pamphlets."

"But not today. The boat sails back to England soon. I must answer the important letters."

"And so must I. Ah, boat days! What joy they bring to us all. Almost, though, they make me homesick. I do not like to admit it, but I do miss England." Mr. Marshman took his letters to his own office.

William's first letter went to Andrew Fuller. He told of the growth of the mission at Serampore, of the splendid men like Marshman and Ward who worked with him in harmony. Then he dared ask a favor: "Please send me Parkhurst's Hebrew and Greek Lexicon, even though I know it costs four guineas. A large door is opened and I have great hope."

When ships were in, company came. Despite anti-missionary rumblings, visitors to Calcutta liked to go up the river to Serampore for tea and conversation. One spring afternoon a stranger in uniform arrived and introduced himself as Captain Kemp. "We haven't met before, sir, but I've brought out so many plants from England for you that I wanted to see you. Lots of them I've kept in my own cabin, and watered myself."

"And how I thank you! The orchid from Wentworth House was in perfect condition, a noble thing. It is in my conservatory now. Would you care to see my precious flowers?"

The two men spent an hour in admiration of choice specimens from England and Asia. As Captain Kemp said good-by, he promised, "If ever I have my own ship, I'll bring out a missionary free of charge."

The Marquess of Wellesley, a brilliant freethinking man, was made the new governor of India. The missionaries at Serampore hoped that he would have a more tolerant attitude toward their work than other officials had had. Soon they felt his friendly, honest spirit.

Each year young men were sent out to India from England to serve in government jobs. When they came, they seldom had any idea of India's geography, language, or customs. The Marquess considered this unfortunate, deplorable. He resolved to open a college where languages would be studied seriously and local religions explained and discussed. Two or three years of such classes would, he was certain, result in better civil servants and promote mutual understanding.

With backing from England and the East India Company, the government set up this college in Calcutta and named it Fort William. An English fort of that name had been built in Calcutta during the earliest years of trade when the English needed protection.

In setting up his faculty, the Marquess asked his chaplain, David Brown, for help. That very afternoon Chaplain Brown took a dhow to Serampore, with news for William Carey. In the garden, as they walked down fragrant paths, he told about his interview with the Marquess.

"I have recommended you to his Excellency, Mr. Carey, to teach Bengali. I told him of your New Testament, just published, of your preaching easily in the language, of your conversations with people in the streets in their own tongue. I can tell you that he was impressed. But he said a funny thing."

"What?"

"He said: 'Carey—isn't he that Baptist?' "

"And—?"

"I admitted it, then praised you for the true Christian spirit you show to all you meet, of whatever religion. You have sincere local respect, sir, as a scholar and as a man."

"That has not always been so. When I arrived in Calcutta, I was unwanted."

"I know, Mr. Carey. The officials of the East India Company have made some mistakes, as most humans do. But they are co-operating in the founding of this college, and you will have their approval now, you may be sure."

William's thoughts raced back to his cobbler shop in

England, where he had taught little boys at night. Teaching had been a means of sharing his knowledge then, and would be so again, if this position was really open.

"Perhaps I should not have come here so quickly, sir," the chaplain said "but I was so happy that I wanted you to be, too. There will be a formal letter of invitation from the Marquess, himself, in tomorrow's post. He is offering you four hundred rupees a year, for three days a week of teaching. I do hope it is enough, and that you will be inclined to accept."

"Enough! I have seldom seen such a sum! Of course I shall say nothing of this until the letter comes, but I shall pray about it tonight."

The morning's mail brought the important letter, as Chaplain Brown had promised.

The whole mission group at Serampore was elated at Carey's appointment. Even Governor Bie was delighted. He made a special trip into Calcutta to congratulate the Marquess for choosing Carey.

It was a splendid change for William to receive so much money at the end of each month. To his surprise, soon after he began to teach, his salary was doubled. One happy day he was able to enclose twenty pounds, as a gift, in a letter to his father in Paulerspury. To his beloved sister Mary, he sent ten pounds. She was his faithful letter writer, giving him word pictures of home that none of his minister-friends ever thought to do. From his salary,

Will put aside a bit to clothe himself properly, but otherwise his money went straight to the mission so its work could grow. The Marshmans' school had taken hold, and it too helped to support the missionaries and pay *pundits* and workers in the mission print shop. Better times were at hand.

William Ward was teaching Felix and William all about printing. They liked to set type and to run errands. They also liked languages. Felix was studying Persian. A Chinese printer had come to live at Serampore. Little Jabez followed him around, ate with chopsticks, and chattered in Chinese to tease his brothers.

"I've a parcel of fruit seeds to take to a ship bound for England this afternoon," Felix told Jabez. "We'll row out. Mummy says you can go with me."

The little *dhow* had one lateen sail, set to catch the wind. Jabez asked the boatmen dozens of questions in Bengali, then he turned to Felix.

"Funny name, Calcutta. Some sailors call it 'Calicut.' Why?"

"Long before we came here, Jabez, Englishmen found three villages near a fine harbor—you can see all the ships, for ten miles around—and close to the temple of Kali. They made a settlement, and first called it 'Kali-cut.' Slowly the name changed to 'Calcutta.' Thus, the name Kalicut, now Calcutta. Kali is the goddess of robbery and murder. Her image holds the head of a giant in one hand

and a sword in another. She wears a necklace of human skulls. I've looked into the temple. It made me know better why Fa' chose to come to tell of Jesus."

"I don't want to hear any more. Kali makes me sick. Now tell me why the Jains wear cloths over their mouths in the streets. I've always wondered."

"That's an easy one. In their religion, they must not kill anything at all. You know how many flies and bugs there are on Calcutta streets. They wear those masks to protect the flies that might get into their mouths and die. Any more whys?"

"One. Why is it that so many Indians won't eat meat? It's good. But my playmates say they can't, they might be eating a grandfather."

"They believe, Jabez, that the same spirit has lots of lives in differing forms. If you are good in this life, you may get a better body in the next. If you are bad, you may move backwards. Some foolish folks think they, or their relatives, may once have been animals. They look at dogs in the street, and wonder if those dogs were their grand-fathers. It's hard for a child to understand. Hard for me, too."

"It's silly."

"Not to them. It's serious. The Bible says that God made man in his own image, but they have no Bibles. They will, though."

The seeds safely delivered, the *dhow* turned to go upriver to Serampore. Faster and faster they sped, for the tide was moving in.

"Hold fast, *sahibs*," commanded the boatman. "We must beat the bore."

They held. The Serampore bore up the Hooghly was well known. Where the river narrowed, the current was strong. During a full moon, tides were always higher than normal. A great wall of water rushed and gushed, once every high tide, with power to overturn a small boat and drown its passengers in a flash. Friends of the Careys were always cautious about the time they paid their visits, lest they be caught in the bore. This boatman knew what he was doing, and the boys were landed safely, though breathless, at the Serampore *ghat*. Their speedy ride made good supper-table conversation.

For convenience, William Carey rented rooms near Fort William College, to stay the three nights a week after his teaching days. There, distinguished gentlemen sought his companionship. So many new friends seemed to approve what the mission was doing at Serampore that it was decided to build a chapel in the heart of wicked Calcutta. A spot at busy Lall Bazar was chosen, and a pretty, dignified church was built. On either side Mr. Carey planted a garden of green shrubs and flame trees to welcome people off the hot dusty road. Businessmen of Calcutta, even non-Christians, gave to help pay for the building. From his own funds, Carey put in a large sum.

From the opening service, it was made clear that in God's house, all were equal. The social system of caste divided all Hindus, outside. They were born, they believed, into a certain group, and in this life could never escape to another. Therefore, Brahman scholars, warriors, craftsmen, merchants, and laborers had nothing to do with one another. Below all of them were the poorest, called "outcastes," who lived a bare, hopeless life. To go together into a house of prayer was at first unthinkable, but as time went by, some did.

Other strangers came—officers and crewmen off boats in harbor, Portuguese residents who were not welcome usually at an English gathering, students in government employ who studied under Carey at Fort William. To them all Carey preached the Great Commission: "Go ye into all the world—" In the city of Calcutta the world was at their dooryard.

One Sunday Carey found a pair of tired-looking shoes tied to the pulpit at Lall Bazar, and knew that someone was trying to remind him of his simple beginnings. Rather than hide the shoes, he held them up and said, "If I, a humble cobbler, could be used of God, how much greater is your opportunity!" And then he remembered the sermon he had preached at Nottingham: "Expect great things from God; attempt great things for God," and repeated it to his congregation of many colors and countries.

His fame spread to America, by letters and from travelers who met him in India. Brown University, of Providence, Rhode Island, conferred on him from its great distance the honorary degree, Doctor of Divinity. From then on, he was known as Dr. Carey.

The Serampore mission grew. Printing presses were added as the translations piled up. For use in England, Dr. Carey wrote *A Garland of Indian Stories*. It was ever his idea to describe one beloved country to the other. Above everything, he wished to interpret his Saviour to those who had never heard of him.

17
"No Thought of Retreat"

Mrs. Dorothy Carey had never found herself at home in India, even in Serampore where there was no crocodile at her door, as there had often been at Mudnabati. For years she closed her eyes to the busy world, and in 1807 she died. Grief was deep within her husband's heart, but he tried to work harder and harder, and to be more of a companion to his boys.

The boys were growing into men.

Felix was talking of becoming a missionary—to China, he hoped—but he was so helpful at the printing presses that he was needed in Serampore. William thought he would go into government service. That pleased his father, for he very much wanted Christians there, and he knew that William would take every opportunity to witness for his Lord.

Carey's days were tightly packed. To his friend John Ryland who had baptized him in the river Nene that cold morning, he sent a copy of a sample day:

Thursday, June 12. Calcutta

5:45–7:00 Dressed. Read a chapter of Hebrew Bible. Devotions.

7:00–10:00 Family worship in Bengali and with the servants. Read Persian with pundit. Revised Scripture proof in Hindustani. Breakfast. Translated portion of the Ramayana from Sanskrit into English.

10:00–1:30 Government college classes.

2:00–6:00 Revised proof of a Jeremiah chapter in Bengali. Translated most of Matthew viii into Sanskrit, with Mrityunjay's help.

6:00–7:00 Tea. Read Telegu with a pundit. A son of Reverend Timothy Thomas of London called.

7:00–9:00 Prepared and preached an English sermon. About forty present, including Judge Harington who afterwards gave sixty-five pounds, ten shillings toward our Calcutta chapel building fund.

9:00–11:00 Translated Ezekiel ii into Bengali. Read a New Testament chapter. Commended myself to God.

Then he apologized: "I never have more time in a day than this."

The years brought many changes.

Governor Bie had a charming cousin at Serampore, Lady Charlotte Rumohr, daughter of a wealthy Danish count. She had come to India for her health, for since childhood, when a fierce fire had swept through her family's castle at home, she had had difficulty walking. Living near the missionaries now, she had become a Baptist, and had given generously to the church. When Krishna Pal had been baptized that momentous morning, Charlotte had been the first to shake his hand in fellowship. Dr. Carey and Lady Charlotte were married.

After this marriage busy years sped by, years of planning and building at Serampore. Dr. Carey and his co-workers decided that they needed a college for Indian students, so they opened one. Beyond Serampore, for all Asia, the Royal Asiatic Society was formed, and William Carey, once a cobbler from Piddington, was invited to be a charter member of this scholarly organization.

By now he even looked like a professor. His hair was white, and he wore it shoulder length, though the top of his head was still bald. Despite the hot climate, he dressed in formal clothes—knee breeches with silver buckles, a full-cut morning coat, and a white linen stock of finest weave wrapped around his neck. He had so much dignity of manner and bearing that taller men, in conversation with him, forgot he was only five feet four, and did not notice that he had to raise his head to meet their eyes. Visitors were often surprised to see an old sign above his desk, which read "Shoes Made and Repaired," but Dr. Carey wanted it there as a permanent reminder of the early troublous months in Bengal.

Not everything was perfect. There were five new graves at Serampore, two of them children of the missionaries. The Marquess of Wellesley had been replaced by a governor-general with no sympathy for mission work. There were grumblings in the city about disturbing pamphlets which were being printed by the mission. Dr. Carey was worried, but as was his custom, he turned his worries over to the Lord and plunged into finishing his *Sanskrit Dictionary*.

The morning of March 12, 1812, Marshman broke into Dr. Carey's Calcutta office unexpectedly, despair so branded on his face that the older man could not imagine what tragedy had put it there.

"Our printing works—fire—burned and naked walls— last night," Marshman burst out, then for a while could say no more.

Dr. Carey was dumb with silence, overwhelmed by the blow.

Gasping for breath and words, Marshman went on, " 'Twas about six last evening, when I heard a shout from Ward. I saw the south end of the long building a twenty-foot sheet of flame. We rushed forward; smoke thrust us back. The window shutters were bolted from within. We fain would have torn them open, but an expert forbade us. Someone did pull one open, and I saw flame leap to the center of the building. We organized carriers, pouring water for four hours, but in another half hour, all was ablaze, and we had then to think of where it might spread."

"And the school?"

"We tried to protect the boys' dormitory, and the girls'.

Luckily we did, for the flame kept straight as a candle. Then there was a crash of beams, and by two o'clock all was spent. At daylight I took the boat to you. The building and its contents have gone. Nothing could have survived such a furnace."

"Was it set? Or an accident?"

"No one knows. We have enemies, 'tis true, but it could easily have come from a worker's pipe. I am needed in Serampore, but I had to bring you the tidings, terrible as they are. I could not bear you to hear it from a stranger."

Dr. Carey bowed his head. "I must be still awhile, and know that the Lord is God," he said. "Then I can go on."

With the inturn of the tide, Carey and Marshman took a boat back to Serampore. Until then, Carey taught his classes at Fort William, and Marshman scoured the shops of Calcutta to see what printing materials were available for purchase.

Down the Hooghly they could smell the smoldering ruins. The building itself was a desolate shell. Ward came running to meet them. His blackened face was creased with smiles as he called out, "All day I have been searching through the debris. I have found four thousand punches of the types of fourteen Indian tongues, more than ten years' labor. And hundreds of pounds of salvageable lead. The paper mill is safe. We can be reprinting within a month." Then his face grew sad. "Dr. Carey, sir, the greatest loss is yours—so many translations: all of your Kanarese New Testament, many pages of the *Bengali Dictionary,* all of the Telugu grammar. Ten thousand pounds may replace our presses and materials, but nothing can replace your work."

Carey heard him out, and replied, "What you have found among the ashes is God's command to us to go forward. We must take heart. My next translations will be better than the old. Let there be no thought of retreat. The Lord has laid me low that I may look more simply to him."

William Ward returned to Serampore one evening after a steaming, rainy day in Calcutta, and asked at once for Dr. Carey. He found him sorting pages of charred manuscript, still hopeful that useable translations could be saved after the fire.

"Why so serious, Brother Ward?"

"Problems, Dr. Carey, but this time not ours."

"We're accustomed to problems, aren't we?"

"Indeed, we are. There's an American couple, Dr. Carey, a Mr. and Mrs. Adoniram Judson, who came to see me at Lall Bazar this morning. They have come as missionaries with some others from their country."

"American missionaries here? It's a splendid cause, but very bad timing. The United States and England are at war on the high seas, and here in Bengal, with the British

East India Company so powerful, Americans will be considered enemy aliens."

"They have discovered that. Moreover, they have a problem of the spirit. They were sent out by the American Board of Commissioners for Foreign Missions, which is Congregational, but on shipboard Mr. Judson became a convinced Baptist. Now he wants to be baptized by immersion. He realizes that this act will sever his connection with his Board in the United States, but his belief is so strong he is willing to face their displeasure. I fear he does not realize the complications of his decision."

Dr. Carey thought a moment, then asked, "And Mrs. Judson?"

"She is troubled. They are anxious to meet you, and ask your advice. I am sure he is sincere."

"Invite them to Serampore early next week. I am happy to welcome American missionaries."

When Ann and Adoniram Judson went to Serampore to meet the great Dr. Carey, they took another young American missionary, Luther Rice. He, also, was an almost-Baptist. The scene in the famous beautiful garden where they had tea was quiet and peaceful, but the conversation was not. The three newcomers were in a dangerous situation.

The East India Company had acted fast, and ordered the Americans to leave, or be arrested and deported to England.

"Have you thought of going to Burma?" inquired Dr. Carey. "My son Felix is there in mission work. He is writing and praying constantly for helpers. You will not be welcomed by the government there, either, but you would probably be permitted to stay."

"Burma. I'll talk with God about it."

"We'll pray now," said Dr. Carey.

At their request, William Ward baptized the three of them in Lall Bazar Chapel, and soon thereafter they escaped down the Hooghly from Calcutta, and on to the Isle of France. To Dr. Carey's satisfaction, the Judsons did sail later to Rangoon, Burma. Luther Rice returned to America, to inform Baptists that they had missionaries in Asia, whether they knew it or not.

18
Darkness to Light

Jabez, a missionary in Rajputana, learned in 1834 that his father was seriously ill, so he hired a boat to take him to Serampore. Caught at night in the Hooghly bore, the boat capsized, and passengers swam for the Barrackpur *ghat*. Indians at the *ghat* pulled them ashore, and when the bore was past, Jabez asked who would take him across the river.

"I, *sahib*," volunteered the master of a tiny *dhow*. "I will take you to Serampore. You are son of the one who has done so much for our country. Not one rupee will you pay. Give me this honor."

An hour later Jabez was asleep in the room he had used as a child, with the same mosquito net tucked around him. Dawn came, and he rose to find his father. He knew that, if he had the strength, Dr. Carey would be at devotions in his beloved garden.

The garden was empty, but the brilliant birds in the aviary knew it was day, and were in full sound. It was a perfect place, declaring what a blending of English and Oriental beauty could become. Presently William Carey came down a path from the house, bent now, and on crutches from a recent fall. In his hand was a Testament.

Father and son greeted each other in tender joy, and sat on a stone bench for prayer. And then they talked, for both of them knew that this might be their last private time together. Dr. Carey had always refused, when he was ill, to stay in bed if he could possibly be in motion. Now, though, his voice was frail, and his skin looked like thin parchment.

"Jabez, have you heard in Rajputana of steamboats? One came from London to Calcutta in sixty-four days! We know the news that happened in England in February, yet it is only April."

"Remarkable. And the news?"

"The Society and other English friends still make gifts toward Indian education and our Bible translations. We have, with their monetary help and our own endeavors, translated the whole Bible into six Indian tongues— Bengali, Oriya, Hindi, Sanskrit, Marathi, and Assamese. You remember the Bengali, how we brought it on the voyage from Mudnabati? After the fire, we did much of our work again, and with God's help, improved it."

"So many people, so far away, have loved you, Fa'."

"And I have loved them. When pounds began to flow in, after our great loss, I noted certain sums from places where I had preached: Northampton, Kettering, Leicester—even fifty pounds from little Moulton. And there was a personal gift of five pounds from a barber, Mr. Wilson, who made my first and only wig, and took me once to call upon William Cowper, the poet. Until that day I had never met a famous man. He gave us tea in his garden. I wish I could invite him here."

While his father rested a moment, Jabez thought of all the smaller Indian languages which Dr. Carey had not named, but on which he had labored with success, of the eighteen far-flung mission centers, stretching from Delhi to Akyab, manned by fifty workers, half pure Indian. He remembered Krishna Pal's baptism, lonely and disturbing to his family, and thought with gratitude of the lively churches now changing darkness to light in Serampore and Calcutta.

In other Indian cities Jabez had, himself, met former students of his father's, now Christians, each of them bearing witness to the Christian faith.

Jabez looked at the small, spent body beside him, and wondered anew at the way God had multiplied his vision. "Expect great things from God; attempt great things for God"—William Carey had lived those words, not just preached them. And his greatest sermon was his own life.

Dr. Carey roused. "Come, Jabez, I've something remarkable to show you." Limping on crutches, he led his son to a border of wild English daisies. "They came, the seeds, in a packet of other things from the garden of an English friend. Odd that I, a country boy, did not know what these were, but I planted them, and none of my rare orchids has given me the pleasure on blooming that these simple daisies did."

He plucked one, and handed it to Jabez, then took another in his hand. "I've something to show you that I only recently observed. There is a special design to a daisy, one of nature's delightful mysteries. Count the florets at the core. The eye sees two distinct sets of spirals, one clockwise, the other counterclockwise. In daisies one set has twenty-one, the other set, thirty-four. That is their pattern. A perfect proportion."

Jabez counted. His father was right.

"To me," said Dr. Carey, "this precision of Nature, even in things she gives us most abundantly, is a proof of the planning of God. If a daisy which grows wild on a hillside is so delicately constructed, how much more wonderful is the human body with its amazing mind. And in turn, the soul which rests in God."

"Yes, Fa'," said Jabez, lamely. There was nothing to add. His father understood nature; he understood the blessings and the commands of God.

Dr. Carey looked wistful for a moment. "You were only an infant when we left England, so you never heard the song of the lark. That is one of the things I have missed most. These daisies help make up for it."

Some years later a young Indian man, dressed in a white *dhoti* and cotton jacket, was seen walking down a lane in Paulerspury. He carried a small Bengali Testament, and it was much worn.

A village man asked where he was going, and whom he sought.

"I have come to see the birthplace of my father," he replied.

"But—," the Englishman was embarrassed to say that no Indian had ever been born here.

The Indian smiled. "I mean my spiritual father, William Carey. He came from Paulerspury, did he not?"

WILLIAM CAREY

Born August 17, 1761
Died June 9, 1834

"The greatest missionary since the Apostle Paul"—so William Carey is often called. Because he was a pioneer in Protestant mission work, students of missions today examine his life and his achievements with special interest.

Poor, obscure, with no influence and little schooling, Carey accomplished almost unbelievable results. He translated the Bible, in whole or in part, into twenty-six Indian languages. He baptized the first Hindu Protestant convert. He and his co-workers were responsible for: the first printing press in India; the first efforts to educate Indian girls and women; the first college to train Indian ministers; the first medical mission in India; the establishment of many mission stations; the first society for the improvement of Indian agriculture; the first translation of the Bible into Sanskrit.

William Carey identified himself with the people of India. He understood their hungers and their needs, and sought for them, through Jesus Christ as Lord, a more abundant life in body, mind, and spirit.